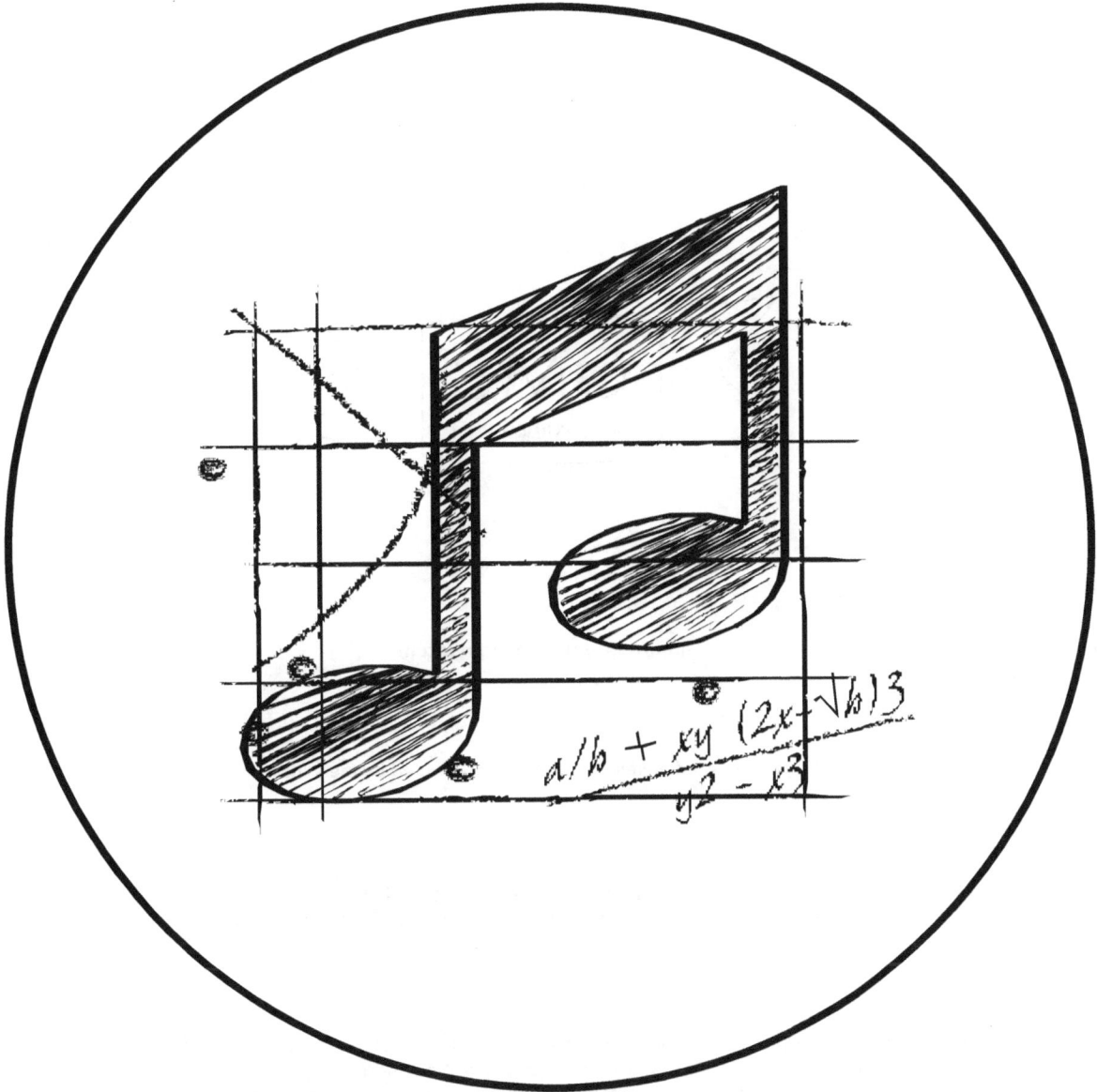

UNABRIDGED DIATONICS SERIES ™

A COMPLETE DIATONIC REFERENCE

THE CIRCLE OF FIFTHS

by

Walter Klosowski III

is published exclusively through:

OMP®
OMNI MUSIC PRESS

OMNI MUSIC PRESS ®

http://www.omnimusicpress.com

Written, designed, edited, compiled, & distributed by the author.

Order Number OMP 002-007

ISBN 978-0692911389

UNABRIDGED DIATONICS SERIES™

For Music

A COMPLETE DIATONIC REFERENCE

THE CIRCLE OF FIFTHS

Walter Klosowski

OMP®
OMNI MUSIC PRESS

Dedicatouilles...

This reference is dedicated to and written for all those who study music, from the casual to the scholar. I am taking this opportunity now to go a bit further than that however, as I need to express a profound thank you to my daughter Halen, my sisters Candas and Laura, and my parents, Walter Jr. & Beverley. All supported me, shared their opinions and insights and simply gave of their time during this project. I would also like to thank my professors, colleagues, students and friends over the years for offering their various opinions and insights as well.

♫

Forward

All the keys of music

Volume seven, like others in the series, is dedicated to showcasing all diatonic material found in all the keys of music that exist on the circle of fifths. This series is the first to fully explore, and subsequently document, all such material in music, as the pages herein list all key signatures, all staple chord progressions and all diatonic chord structures in all keys, major and minor. This volume is divided into four respective chapters, those being, the sharp major keys, the flat major keys, the sharp minor keys and the flat minor keys.

The diatonic realm

It has long been recognized that music is, by nature, infinite; its twelve notes combined with the various rhythms are truly inexaustable. The *diatonic realm* is defined here as that material in music which is taken from this infinite, as all diatonic material is essentially finite. Oddly, the material in the realm remains musical, yet has an end. And because of this trait, it is the only material in music subject to full documentation. For that is, essentially, the service this reference provides, as all that exists in the diatonic realm remains its only focus. From the most frequently used key signatures, to the common chord progressions, from every diatonic triad chord, to every color tone, seventh chord and extenstion, all is captured right here in all keys, major and minor.

Circle of fifths

Each key depicted in this volume can likewise be found on music's ever popular circle of fifths. This volume features the circle too, as it is depicted on the left hand page. All the keys are present and accounted for there, listed by chapter, sharp or flat, major or minor, as is the extent of this volume. The first key on the top of the circle in the opening chapter is the key of C major.

This reference does not go into detailed explanations as to the various concepts associated with music forms. But the one musical concept it does promote is the spacing of the keys a perfect fifth apart. The reason behind having the keys spaced this way coresponds to the successive order of the seven accidentals for each key as seen on the circle itself. This reference is based on this same order, giving each individual key its own dedicated chapter. There are no musical shortcuts, as all information presented here is done so without needless explotation of the enharmonic equavilent keys. In this reference, each individual key receives identical treatment when presented.

Hint. When selecting the particular key from the chapters use the darkened oval bullet as featured. It quickly singles out which one of the keys is the actual chosen key at hand. And as a bonus, just underneath the vertical title on the left hand page where the circle is, one finds the scale of the given key as well.

A word about the key signature of C major and A minor. Although not a sharp or flat key, the key itself, or more specifically the signature, is included with the other key groups because it remains the only signature free of accidentals. This unique quality makes for an ideal beginning and ending point for this and other music projects.

CLEFS & KEY SIGNATURES

The material on the left hand page is purposefully designed to coordinate with the material found on the right hand page. Glancing atop the right hand page, one finds an in depth, highly detailed look at some four different clefs and how the key signature of the given major or minor key appears on each. The four clefs featured atop the right hand page are the treble, bass, alto and tenor. All of them are presented below as they are found in the actual text. The given key signature is depicted on each of them. Most musicians make use of key signatures at some point, as each clef and signature showcased is quite unique to music notation.

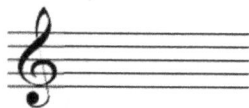

| Treble | Bass | Alto | Tenor |

Of all the clefs used in music notation, the treble clef is often the one first introduced and easily recognized. Also called the G clef, it is used for the violin, the guitar, most woodwinds and the high brass. This clef, generally speaking, is used to signify the right hand in keyboard literature. The next clef in line is the bass clef, and it is easily recognized by a fair number of musicians just the same. Often called the F clef, it is used for the double bass, electric string bass and the lower brass instruments. This clef, generally speaking, is used to signify the left hand in keyboard literature. The remaining two clefs, alto and tenor, are related to each other. The alto clef is considered a movable C clef and is typically used for the viola. Since most instruments do not regularly use this clef, it is not always immediately recognized. The tenor clef is likewise considered to be a movable C clef, hence the relation, and it is used for the cello, bassoon and trombone.

When learning about key signatures it is important to bear in mind three things; the actual clef in use, the orientation of the accidentals on the lines and spaces of the staff, and the specific number of accidentals that the given key requires. All three things are combined together and all are very important to muisc notation. Also remember that any single signature actually implies two keys, one being major and the other minor. The keys are related to each other on the circle as found. Such information is commonly discussed in the music theory texts for further study. It seems by examination of the written manuscript in question, looking at the music notation or playing through it if possible, are some of the ways used to determine which key is being used.

CHORD PROGRESSIONS

On down the page, just below the key signature material, one finds a listing of common chord progressions used in the given key. All progressions showcased are done so exclusively in the diatonic realm (no borrowed chords) and all material presented in this volume is done so using a non-notation, visually based format. When studying these, keep in mind the subtle role of personal opinion embedded within the musical choices regarding chord progressions. Amongst the infinite number of chords available from which to progress, what seems rather commonplace to one musician may or may not be considered as such by another. Plus one's intellectual capacity for chord knowledge is constantly evolving. Such an ever developing working knowledge of the subject coupled with a multitude of compositional choices leads to different ideas as to what constitutes musically effective chord progressions.

That said, certain chord progressions have evolved over time to become a staple in the art of music composition. A list of these commonly used progressions is presented below in the proverbial key of C major.

$I \Rightarrow V \Rightarrow I$ ...	implies ...	C Maj $\Rightarrow$ G Maj $\Rightarrow$ C Maj...
$iii \Rightarrow V \Rightarrow I$ ...	implies ...	e min $\Rightarrow$ G Maj $\Rightarrow$ C Maj...
$I \Rightarrow IV \Rightarrow V \Rightarrow I$ ...	implies ...	C Maj $\Rightarrow$ C Maj $\Rightarrow$ G Maj $\Rightarrow$ C Maj...
$I \Rightarrow ii \Rightarrow V \Rightarrow I$ ...	implies ...	C Maj $\Rightarrow$ d min $\Rightarrow$ G Maj $\Rightarrow$ C Maj...
$I \Rightarrow vi \Rightarrow ii \Rightarrow V$ ...	implies ...	C Maj $\Rightarrow$ a min $\Rightarrow$ d min $\Rightarrow$ G Maj...
$iii \Rightarrow vi \Rightarrow ii \Rightarrow V$ ...	implies ...	e min $\Rightarrow$ a min $\Rightarrow$ d min $\Rightarrow$ G Maj...

All roman numerals found in the diatonic progressions chart listed above are placed directly across from their chord name counterpart in this, and every other, example found in this text. All progression nomenclature showcased in this book is taken from music notation, point in case with its inclusion of roman numerals and chord names. The little line found to the left of the example is simply meant to draw attention to those progressions that use the primary chords, and the arrow ($\Rightarrow$) symbol, which is placed in between the roman numerals and chords, symbolizes the flow of time between the chords as they progress to and from one another. Notice the purposeful sensitivity towards upper and lower case letter use in the above example. This is an important detail as the upper case implies the major chord quality while the lower case implies the minor. Other music notation based nomenclature detail is likewise reflected in this example.

These progressions have become very common, a staple, in the art as they serve the purposes of music composition very well and are heavily relied upon during the composition process. Their prevalence amongst a variety of music styles is due mostly to their effectiveness, generally speaking, in the given musical situation.

Also, when studying chord progression material, notice that the roman numeral nomenclature itself stays the same as one moves from key to key. Contrast that against the implied diatonic chords found in each of those keys, for they constantly change with every new sharp or flat major key selected. This concept is easily demonstrated by flipping through the pages of this book.

DIATONIC CHORD STRUCTURE

Lastly, by turning the page, one finds the unabridged diatonic chord structure grid for the given sharp or flat major key at hand, thus defining the diatonic realm as found in this reference. The diatonic material found here in this section is divided into four areas of tonality, which are, respectively, the triad chords, their color tones, the seventh chords, and their extensions. Studying diatonic chord structure is arguably one of the more important things to do because a developed working knowledge of it leads to a better overall understanding of the composition process. This eventual accumulation of knowledge also leads to a solid understanding of the non-diatonic as well. The materials found here in this volume are purposely designed to support this learning curve.

In order to present this amount of information in a very practical manner, it became necessary to place it on a grid of sorts, like a picture snapshot. Take a look at the following example below.

$6^{th}/13^{th}$
$4^{th}/11^{th}$
$2^{nd}/9^{th}$

$/7^{th}$

5th ...
3rd ...
Root...

| I | ii | iii | IV | V | vi | $vii°$ | I |

The example is empty at the moment, exposing the *x* and *y* axis for the purposes of explanation. It is essential to understand what the *x* and *y* axis imply when used individually or together. The roman numerals on the *x* axis are discussed first.

The roman numerals placed across the bottom of the grid (*x* axis) represent all of the available diatonic chords as found in the given sharp or flat major key. The alphanumeric numerals, placed vertically up the side (*y* axis), represent all the individual notes that constitute the structure for all diatonic chords as found in the given sharp or flat major key. All diatonic chord structures in the grid place the root at the bottom with the thirteenth at the top. Using roman numerals in combination with alpha numeric in this manner has a very powerful impact on the user. This grid (*x* & *y* axis) is featured throughout the book and showcases everything in the diatonic realm for the given key at hand. That diatonic breakdown is further discussed in the following paragraphs.

TRIADS

In this music reference, the diatonic triad chords are the first tonal area to be presented. The example below showcases all diatonic triads in the key of C major.

5th ...	G	A	B	C	D	E	F	G
3rd ...	E	F	G	A	B	C	D	E
Root...	C	D	E	F	G	A	B	C
	I	*ii*	*iii*	*IV*	*V*	*vi*	*vii°*	*I*

The example places all the roots at the bottom, with the third degree in the middle, and the fifth degree atop that. Their proper terms are presented below.

- the tonic (I), or the "major one triad" chord
- the supertonic (ii), or the "minor two triad" chord
- the mediant (iii), the "minor three triad" chord
- the subdominant (IV), the "major four or subdominant triad" chord
- the dominant (V), the "major five or dominant triad" chord
- the submediant (vi), the "minor six triad" chord
- the leading tone (vii°), the "seven diminished triad" chord

The small line, placed next to the triads, is meant to highlight their presence on the grid. In this reference, the word *triad* implies a tertian chord structure as based in equal tempered tuning. Considered rather commonplace in the study, triads are found in nearly all styles of music and all are considered musically valid in the art. All of the triads found in the example are encountered early in the study of music theory and, from the material provided one can easily see the intimate structure of each chord found in the given sharp or flat major key. Also when dealing with triads, it is permissible to omit the fifth note from the triad chord voicing from time to time. Oddly, as it is found in the music literature, the fifth note does not always need to be present to obtain the triad sonority. When encountered in music, it is sometimes called a dyad, and they are popular amongst string players.

COLOR TONES

The color tones, as showcased here, are often voiced with triads. And because of that they represent the next bit of diatonic material to be dealt with here.

6th	A	B	C	D	E	F	G	A
4th	F	G	A	B	C	D	E	F
2nd	D	E	F	G	A	B	C	D
5th ...	G	A	B	C	D	E	F	G
3rd ...	E	F	G	A	B	C	D	E
Root...	C	D	E	F	G	A	B	C
	I	ii	iii	IV	V	vi	vii°	I

Color tones are meant to be added to the triad voicing, but do not necessarily replace any of those said triad notes. In this reference, a *color tone* is defined as any single diatonic note, below the seventh, added to the actual triad voicing. Simply voice the triad and put this extra note in when needed. Though four notes are present, the chord sonority itself is still considered a triad nonetheless. Generally speaking there can be a duplication of a note from the triad, but usually the color tone itself is not doubled in the voicing. The seventh is not present, and more than one color tone may be added. Composers often fuse color tones into their work to increase harmonic interest as color tones enrich the chord sonority itself.

As this reference shows, each given triad has at least three formal diatonic color tones from which to choose; the second, the fourth and the sixth. The second scale degree is often placed alongside the root, as that sonority is very pleasing to the ear.

When the fourth scale degree replaces the third scale degree in music, the triad is said to be suspended. Take any given triad and add the sixth to it; a darker sonority emerges. Adding color tones also can result in a chromatic chord voicing, meaning a color tone or two is played simultaneously with the triad voicing while omitting nothing from the triad itself. A good example of this would be the suspended four with the third still voiced.

SEVENTHS

The grid below shows all diatonic seventh chords found in the key of C major. Taking notes from the diatonic chords and changing them up a bit is nothing new in music, but understand that notes must remain the same. Any additional raising or lowering of the diatonic notes presented below is considered a step outside the key, for all seventh chords presented here, and all others in this reference, are done so in their natural diatonic state without any alteration.

7th	B	C	D	E	F	G	A	B
5th ...	G	A	B	C	D	E	F	G
3rd ...	E	F	G	A	B	C	D	E
Root...	C	D	E	F	G	A	B	C
	$I^{\Delta 7}$	ii^7	iii^7	$IV^{\Delta 7}$	V^7	vi^7	$vii^{\emptyset 7}$	$I^{\Delta 7}$

Seventh chords are in contrast to color tones because adding a color tone to a triad does not change said triad into another chord type. One simply adds the seventh note to a triad voicing, true, but the addition of the seventh note is what creates a whole new different chord type, the *seventh chord*. Seventh chords are musically complex due in part to their resolution issues and other voice leading implications.

- the tonic seventh ($I^{\Delta 7}$), or the "major one, major seventh" chord
- the supertonic seventh (ii^7), the "minor two, seventh" chord
- the mediant seventh (iii^7), the "minor three, seventh" chord
- the subdominant seventh ($IV^{\Delta 7}$), the "major four, major seventh" chord
- the dominant seventh (V^7), the "major five, minor or dominant seventh" chord
- the submediant seventh (vi^7), the "minor six, seventh" chord
- the leading tone seventh ($vii^{\emptyset 7}$), the "seven, half diminished seventh" chord

The five seventh chord (V ^{7}) is of particular importance as it has certain treatments of its third and seventh degree that are considered standard in the art. These specific resolutions are thoroughly explored and fully discussed in most any music theory text. All seventh chords are likewise presented for all remaining major and minor keys in this volume.

CHORD EXTENSIONS

Composers of all kinds have long incorporated extensions into their seventh chords, mostly for voice leading purposes, but also to increase harmonic interest or increase/decrease melodic tension, or possibly to enrich the given chord sonority itself. Whatever the reason, as this reference shows, each given seventh chord has at least three diatonic extension notes from which to choose, as seen in the example below.

13th	A	B	C	D	E	F	G	A
11th	F	G	A	B	C	D	E	F
9th	D	E	F	G	A	B	C	D
7th	B	C	D	E	F	G	A	B
5th ...	G	A	B	C	D	E	F	G
3rd ...	E	F	G	A	B	C	D	E
Root...	C	D	E	F	G	A	B	C
	$I^{\triangle 7}$	ii^7	iii^7	$IV^{\triangle 7}$	V^7	vi^7	$vii^{\emptyset 7}$	$I^{\triangle 7}$

The term *chord extensions*, as showcased here in the key of C major, refers to those diatonic notes located above the seventh. When one uses extensions in chord work, generally speaking, the seventh note itself is not usually duplicated. However, the chord typically includes the seventh and one or more notes beyond the seventh, as the chart diatonically shows. There are three chord extension notes from which to choose, and they are formally called the ninth, the eleventh and the thirteenth. The seventh note itself is of particular importance here, as the extension note itself must be voiced together with it in the actual sonority, otherwise the chord itself cannot be nor is extended. Simply adding one or more of these diatonic notes to an already existing seventh chord is all that is required to play them. That said, when voicing extensions, it is typical to place the extended notes above the seventh note, but this is not always the case in actual music. What is clear though is the combination of the two, the seventh combined with the extension. More than one extension note may be added to any seventh chord voicing without replacing any other notes and the fifth can be omitted at any time.

CLOSING

It is interesting to point out that the music material in this reference does not rely on music notation. This is because music notation, though a universal language used and accepted, is not always the best thing to turn to when explaining music theory and composition. The material found in this reference, however, does indeed reflect on the nomenclature quite a bit. For example, notice the deliberate use of both the upper and lower case roman numerals on the grid, as well as the alpha numeric use, not to mention the various chord signia, clefs and the key signatures too. All of this is found in music notation and has likewise been transferred over to the material found in this reference here.

Music notation has long been the standard language composers use to convey the various sounds and silences within their compositions. Though it may have its challenges from time to time, it has endured, and nearly all musicians are expected to learn it at some point. Music teachers often debate that scholarly works from the music repertoire should serve as the only resource of study, sometimes to the exclusion of all others. And because those sources are written in notation, it forces the entry level student to deal with the music language right away. Musical works like J. S. Bach's *Well Tempered Clavier* or his *Art of the Fugue* are popular with music theorists because of their exemplary musical qualities regarding melody, form, chord voicings etc., all of which have stood the test of time and are simply too are valuable to be denied.

It is true that classical works from the repertoire do traditionally function as the sole resource for study, but it is here that an important distinction must be made. Notation is best used to communicate the written music, yes, but again it is not necessarily the best tool to use when it comes to explaining certain concepts on an instrument per say. In some situations music notation can actually be quite difficult looking when written out yet simple to play. This poses a frustrating situation for the absolute beginner who is often eager to learn, but becomes discouraged when decifering the embedded musical hieroglyphs and does not see the overall bigger musical picture that is unfolding in the composition. True, learning how to read music can be frustrating, especially for the beginning student who, in all likelyhood, is not familiar enough to be diciphering its nomenclature correctly. And given this, plus the task of learning the pending implications associated with music analysis, it is understandable how the learning situation can be. Not to mention, misinformation.

It is here at this precipice where the advantages of knowing first the diatonic material emerge and become clear. And hence the reason for a series of music references such as this, one that is inclusive to all keys, delineates the entire diatonic realm and allows for everyone to see what is going on musically. Presenting the diatonic musical material in a way that is outside notation allows the series to work in conjuction with music theory textbooks, workbooks and other print music subject matter as well. Considering the vastness of the subject area, this diatonic music reference proves itself to be a reliable powerhouse of musical information, a fine compliment to one's music library.

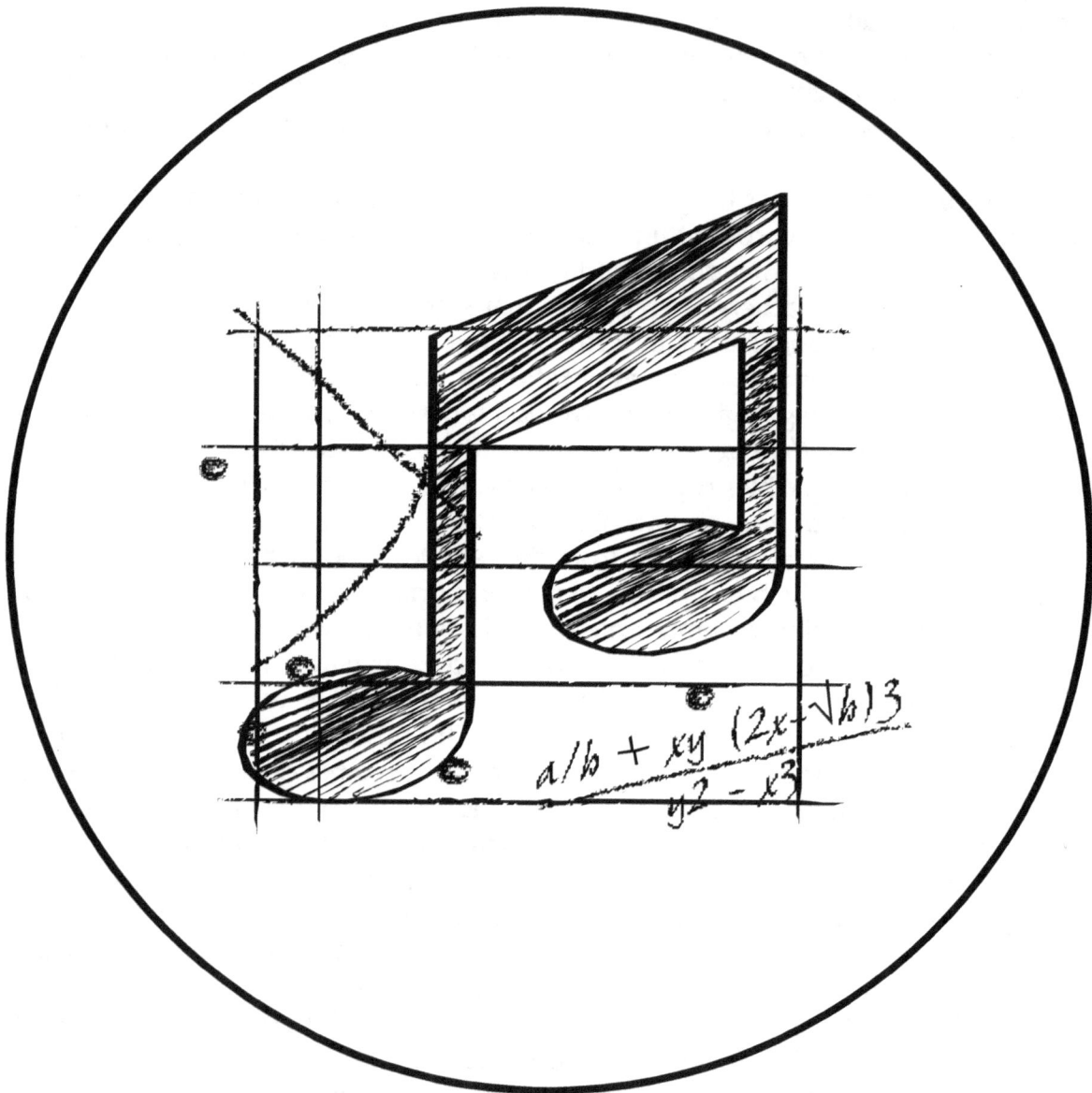

C Major	04		Cb Major	38
G Major	08		Gb Major	42
D Major	12		Db Major	46
A Major	16		Ab Major	50
E Major	20		Eb Major	54
B Major	24		Bb Major	58
F# Major	28		F Major	62
C# Major	32		C Major	66

A Minor	72
E Minor	76
B Minor	80
F# Minor	84
C# Minor	88
G# Minor	92
D# Minor	96
A# Minor	100

A♭ Minor	106
E♭ Minor	110
B♭ Minor	114
F Minor	118
C Minor	122
G Minor	126
D Minor	130
A Minor	134

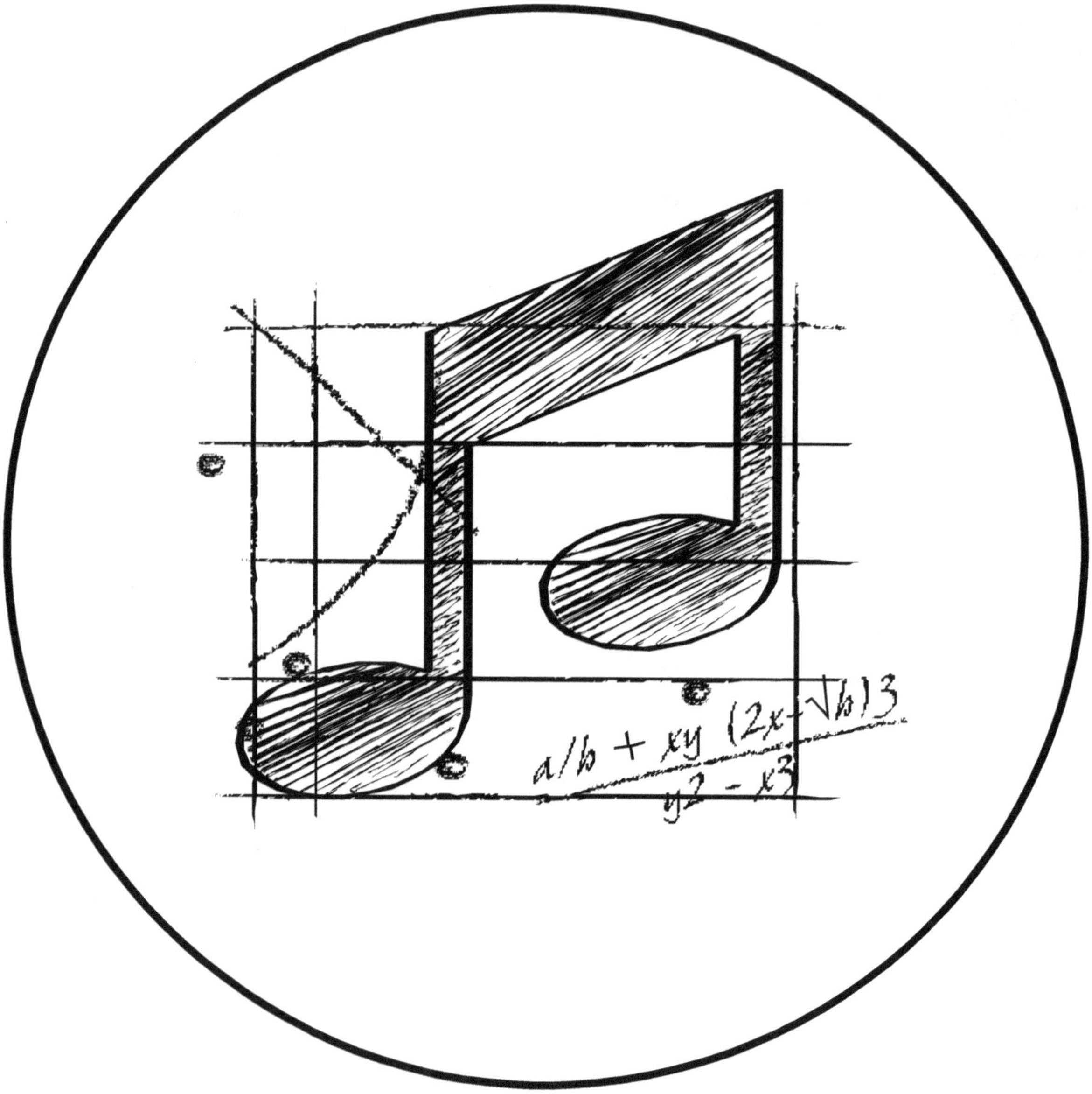
a/b + xy (2x-√b)3
y2 - x3

CHAPTER ONE

The Sharp Major Keys

C Major ^{0 Sharps}

G Major ^{1 Sharp}

D Major ^{2 Sharps}

A Major ^{3 Sharps}

E Major ^{4 Sharps}

B Major ^{5 Sharps}
C♭ **Enharmonic Equivalent**

F♯ Major ^{6 Sharps}
G♭ **Enharmonic Equivalent**

C♯ Major ^{7 Sharps}
D♭ **Enharmonic Equivalent**

The Key of C Major

The C major scale uses the notes C, D, E, F, G, A, B & C.

The Key of C Major

implies -- C, D, E, F, G, A & B.

Signature

CLEFS & KEY SIGNATURE

Treble or G clef...

Alto or movable C clef...

Bass or F clef...

Tenor or movable C clef...

♪ The C major key signature has no sharps or flats.

Progressions

COMMON PROGRESSIONS

I ⇨ V ⇨ I ...	implies ...	C Maj ⇨ G Maj ⇨ C Maj...
iii ⇨ V ⇨ I ...	implies ...	e min ⇨ G Maj ⇨ C Maj...
I ⇨ IV ⇨ V ⇨ I ...	implies ...	C Maj ⇨ C Maj ⇨ G Maj ⇨ C Maj...
I ⇨ ii ⇨ V ⇨ I ...	implies ...	C Maj ⇨ d min ⇨ G Maj ⇨ C Maj...
I ⇨ vi ⇨ ii ⇨ V...	implies ...	C Maj ⇨ a min ⇨ d min ⇨ G Maj...
iii ⇨ vi ⇨ ii ⇨ V...	implies ...	e min ⇨ a min ⇨ d min ⇨ G Maj...

♪ The primary chords are C major ^{Tonic}, F major ^{Subdominant} & G major ^{Dominant}.

C Triads & Color Tones

The key of A minor is...

Color Tones
DIATONIC CHORD STRUCTURE

6th	A	B	C	D	E	F	G	A
4th	F	G	A	B	C	D	E	F
2nd	D	E	F	G	A	B	C	D
5th ...	G	A	B	C	D	E	F	G
3rd ...	E	F	G	A	B	C	D	E
Root...	C	D	E	F	G	A	B	C
	I	ii	iii	IV	V	vi	vii°	I

♪ Any color tone or tones may be voiced with the given triad chord.

Triads
DIATONIC CHORD STRUCTURE

5th ...	G	A	B	C	D	E	F	G
3rd ...	E	F	G	A	B	C	D	E
Root...	C	D	E	F	G	A	B	C
	I	ii	iii	IV	V	vi	vii°	I

♪ A triad chord is commonly voiced using just the root & third.

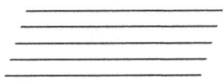

C Sevenths & Extensions

...relative to the key of C major.

Extensions
DIATONIC CHORD STRUCTURE

13th	A	B	C	D	E	F	G	A
11th	F	G	A	B	C	D	E	F
9th	D	E	F	G	A	B	C	D
7th	B	C	D	E	F	G	A	B
5th ...	G	A	B	C	D	E	F	G
3rd ...	E	F	G	A	B	C	D	E
Root...	C	D	E	F	G	A	B	C
	$I^{\triangle 7}$	ii^7	iii^7	$IV^{\triangle 7}$	V^7	vi^7	$vii^{\varnothing 7}$	$I^{\triangle 7}$

♪ Any extension or extensions may be voiced with the given seventh chord.

Sevenths
DIATONIC CHORD STRUCTURE

7th	B	C	D	E	F	G	A	B
5th ...	G	A	B	C	D	E	F	G
3rd ...	E	F	G	A	B	C	D	E
Root...	C	D	E	F	G	A	B	C
	$I^{\triangle 7}$	ii^7	iii^7	$IV^{\triangle 7}$	V^7	vi^7	$vii^{\varnothing 7}$	$I^{\triangle 7}$

♪ A seventh chord is commonly voiced using just the root, third & seventh.

UNABRIDGED DIATONICS™ A COMPLETE DIATONIC REFERENCE – THE CIRCLE OF FIFTHS COPYRIGHT © 2011 OMNI MUSIC PRESS®

C Major ⁰ Sharps

G Major ¹ Sharp

D Major ² Sharps

A Major ³ Sharps

E Major ⁴ Sharps

B Major ⁵ Sharps
C♭ Enharmonic Equivalent

F♯ Major ⁶ Sharps
G♭ Enharmonic Equivalent

C♯ Major ⁷ Sharps
D♭ Enharmonic Equivalent

The Key of G Major
The G major scale uses the notes G, A, B, C, D E, F♯ & G.

The Key of G Major

implies -- G, A, B, C, D, E & F♯.

Signature

CLEFS & KEY SIGNATURE

Treble or G clef...

Alto or movable C clef...

Bass or F clef...

Tenor or movable C clef...

♫ The G major key signature has one sharp -- F♯.

Progressions

COMMON PROGRESSIONS

I ⇨ V ⇨ I ...	implies	...	G Maj ⇨ D Maj ⇨ G Maj...
iii ⇨ V ⇨ I ...	implies	...	b min ⇨ D Maj ⇨ G Maj...
I ⇨ IV ⇨ V ⇨ I ...	implies	...	G Maj ⇨ C Maj ⇨ D Maj ⇨ G Maj...
I ⇨ ii ⇨ V ⇨ I ...	implies	...	G Maj ⇨ a min ⇨ D Maj ⇨ G Maj...
I ⇨ vi ⇨ ii ⇨ V...	implies	...	G Maj ⇨ e min ⇨ a min ⇨ D Maj...
iii ⇨ vi ⇨ ii ⇨ V...	implies	...	b min ⇨ e min ⇨ a min ⇨ D Maj...

♫ The primary chords are G major ᵀᵒⁿⁱᶜ, C major ˢᵘᵇᵈᵒᵐⁱⁿᵃⁿᵗ & D major ᴰᵒᵐⁱⁿᵃⁿᵗ.

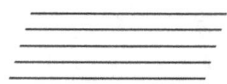

G Triads & Color Tones

The key of E minor is...

Color Tones
DIATONIC CHORD STRUCTURE

6th	E	F#	G	A	B	C	D	E
4th	C	D	E	F#	G	A	B	C
2nd	A	B	C	D	E	F#	G	A
5th ...	D	E	F#	G	A	B	C	D
3rd ...	B	C	D	E	F#	G	A	B
Root...	G	A	B	C	D	E	F#	G
	I	ii	iii	IV	V	vi	vii°	I

♫ Any color tone or tones may be voiced with the given triad chord.

Triads
DIATONIC CHORD STRUCTURE

5th ...	D	E	F#	G	A	B	C	D
3rd ...	B	C	D	E	F#	G	A	B
Root...	G	A	B	C	D	E	F#	G
	I	ii	iii	IV	V	vi	vii°	I

♫ A triad chord is commonly voiced using just the root & third.

G Sevenths & Extensions

...relative to the key of G major.

E x t e n s i o n s
DIATONIC CHORD STRUCTURE

13th	E	F#	G	A	B	C	D	E
11th	C	D	E	F#	G	A	B	C
9th	A	B	C	D	E	F#	G	A
7th	F#	G	A	B	C	D	E	F#
5th ...	D	E	F#	G	A	B	C	D
3rd ...	B	C	D	E	F#	G	A	B
Root...	G	A	B	C	D	E	F#	G
	$I^{\triangle 7}$	ii^7	iii^7	$IV^{\triangle 7}$	V^7	vi^7	$vii^{\o 7}$	$I^{\triangle 7}$

♫ Any extension or extensions may be voiced with the given seventh chord.

S e v e n t h s
DIATONIC CHORD STRUCTURE

7th	F#	G	A	B	C	D	E	F#
5th ...	D	E	F#	G	A	B	C	D
3rd ...	B	C	D	E	F#	G	A	B
Root...	G	A	B	C	D	E	F#	G
	$I^{\triangle 7}$	ii^7	iii^7	$IV^{\triangle 7}$	V^7	vi^7	$vii^{\o 7}$	$I^{\triangle 7}$

♫ A seventh chord is commonly voiced using just the root, third & seventh.

C Major ^{0 Sharps}

G Major ^{1 Sharp}

D Major ^{2 Sharps}

A Major ^{3 Sharps}

E Major ^{4 Sharps}

B Major ^{5 Sharps}
C♭ Enharmonic Equivalent

F♯ Major ^{6 Sharps}
G♭ Enharmonic Equivalent

C♯ Major ^{7 Sharps}
D♭ Enharmonic Equivalent

The Key of D Major
The D major scale uses the notes D, E, F♯, G, A, B, C♯ & D.

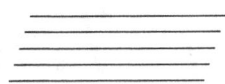

The Key of D Major

implies -- D, E, F♯, G, A, B & C♯.

Signature

CLEFS & KEY SIGNATURE

Treble or G clef...

Alto or movable C clef...

Bass or F clef...

Tenor or movable C clef...

♫ The D major key signature has two sharps -- F♯ & C♯.

Progressions

COMMON PROGRESSIONS

I ⇨ V ⇨ I ...	implies ...	D Maj ⇨ A Maj ⇨ D Maj...
iii ⇨ V ⇨ I ...	implies ...	f♯ min ⇨ A Maj ⇨ D Maj...
I ⇨ IV ⇨ V ⇨ I ...	implies ...	D Maj ⇨ G Maj ⇨ A Maj ⇨ D Maj...
I ⇨ ii ⇨ V ⇨ I ...	implies ...	D Maj ⇨ e min ⇨ A Maj ⇨ D Maj...
I ⇨ vi ⇨ ii ⇨ V ...	implies ...	D Maj ⇨ b min ⇨ e min ⇨ A Maj...
iii ⇨ vi ⇨ ii ⇨ V ...	implies ...	f♯ min ⇨ b min ⇨ e min ⇨ A Maj...

♫ The primary chords are D major ᵀᵒⁿⁱᶜ, G major ˢᵘᵇᵈᵒᵐⁱⁿᵃⁿᵗ & A major ᴰᵒᵐⁱⁿᵃⁿᵗ.

D Triads & Color Tones

The key of B minor is...

Color Tones

DIATONIC CHORD STRUCTURE

6th	B	C#	D	E	F#	G	A	B
4th	G	A	B	C#	D	E	F#	G
2nd	E	F#	G	A	B	C#	D	E
5th ...	A	B	C#	D	E	F#	G	A
3rd ...	F#	G	A	B	C#	D	E	F#
Root...	D	E	F#	G	A	B	C#	D
	I	*ii*	*iii*	*IV*	*V*	*vi*	*vii°*	*I*

♫ Any color tone or tones may be voiced with the given triad chord.

Triads

DIATONIC CHORD STRUCTURE

5th ...	A	B	C#	D	E	F#	G	A
3rd ...	F#	G	A	B	C#	D	E	F#
Root...	D	E	F#	G	A	B	C#	D
	I	*ii*	*iii*	*IV*	*V*	*vi*	*vii°*	*I*

♫ A triad chord is commonly voiced using just the root & third.

D Sevenths & Extensions

...relative to the key of D major.

Extensions
DIATONIC CHORD STRUCTURE

13th	B	C#	D	E	F#	G	A	B
11th	G	A	B	C#	D	E	F#	G
9th	E	F#	G	A	B	C#	D	E
7th	C#	D	E	F#	G	A	B	C#
5th ...	A	B	C#	D	E	F#	G	A
3rd ...	F#	G	A	B	C#	D	E	F#
Root...	D	E	F#	G	A	B	C#	D
	$I^{\triangle 7}$	ii^7	iii^7	$IV^{\triangle 7}$	V^7	vi^7	$vii^{\o 7}$	$I^{\triangle 7}$

♪ Any extension or extensions may be voiced with the given seventh chord.

Sevenths
DIATONIC CHORD STRUCTURE

7th	C#	D	E	F#	G	A	B	C#
5th ...	A	B	C#	D	E	F#	G	A
3rd ...	F#	G	A	B	C#	D	E	F#
Root...	D	E	F#	G	A	B	C#	D
	$I^{\triangle 7}$	ii^7	iii^7	$IV^{\triangle 7}$	V^7	vi^7	$vii^{\o 7}$	$I^{\triangle 7}$

♪ A seventh chord is commonly voiced using just the root, third & seventh.

C Major ^{0 Sharps}

G Major ^{1 Sharp}

D Major ^{2 Sharps}

A Major ^{3 Sharps}

E Major ^{4 Sharps}

B Major ^{5 Sharps}
C♭ Enharmonic Equivalent

F♯ Major ^{6 Sharps}
G♭ Enharmonic Equivalent

C♯ Major ^{7 Sharps}
D♭ Enharmonic Equivalent

The Key of A Major

The A major scale uses the notes A, B, C♯, D, E, F♯, G♯ & A.

The Key of A Major

implies -- A, B, C#, D, E, F# & G#.

Signature

CLEFS & KEY SIGNATURE

Treble or G clef...

Alto or movable C clef...

Bass or F clef...

Tenor or movable C clef...

♫ The A major key signature has three sharps -- F#, C#, & G#.

Progressions

COMMON PROGRESSIONS

I ⇨ V ⇨ I ...	implies ...	A Maj ⇨ E Maj ⇨ A Maj...
iii ⇨ V ⇨ I ...	implies ...	c# min ⇨ E Maj ⇨ A Maj...
I ⇨ IV ⇨ V ⇨ I ...	implies ...	A Maj ⇨ D Maj ⇨ E Maj ⇨ A Maj...
I ⇨ ii ⇨ V ⇨ I ...	implies ...	A Maj ⇨ b min ⇨ E Maj ⇨ A Maj...
I ⇨ vi ⇨ ii ⇨ V...	implies ...	A Maj ⇨ f# min ⇨ b min ⇨ E Maj...
iii ⇨ vi ⇨ ii ⇨ V...	implies ...	c# min ⇨ f# min ⇨ b min ⇨ E Maj...

♫ The primary chords are A major ^{Tonic}, D major ^{Subdominant} & E major ^{Dominant}.

A Triads & Color Tones

The key of F# minor is...

Color Tones

DIATONIC CHORD STRUCTURE

6th	F#	G#	A	B	C#	D	E	F#
4th	D	E	F#	G#	A	B	C#	D
2nd	B	C#	D	E	F#	G#	A	B
5th ...	E	F#	G#	A	B	C#	D	E
3rd ...	C#	D	E	F#	G#	A	B	C#
Root...	A	B	C#	D	E	F#	G#	A
	I	ii	iii	IV	V	vi	vii°	I

♪ Any color tone or tones may be voiced with the given triad chord.

Triads

DIATONIC CHORD STRUCTURE

5th ...	E	F#	G#	A	B	C#	D	E
3rd ...	C#	D	E	F#	G#	A	B	C#
Root...	A	B	C#	D	E	F#	G#	A
	I	ii	iii	IV	V	vi	vii°	I

♪ A triad chord is commonly voiced using just the root & third.

A Sevenths & Extensions

...relative to the key of A major.

Extensions

DIATONIC CHORD STRUCTURE

13th	F#	G#	A	B	C#	D	E	C#
11th	D	E	F#	G#	A	B	C#	D
9th	B	C#	D	E	F#	G#	A	F#
7th	G#	A	B	C#	D	E	F#	G#
5th ...	E	F#	G#	A	B	C#	D	E
3rd ...	C#	D	E	F#	G#	A	B	C#
Root...	A	B	C#	D	E	F#	G#	A
	$I^{\Delta 7}$	ii^7	iii^7	$IV^{\Delta 7}$	V^7	vi^7	$vii^{\o 7}$	$I^{\Delta 7}$

♫ Any extension or extensions may be voiced with the given seventh chord.

Sevenths

DIATONIC CHORD STRUCTURE

7th	G#	A	B	C#	D	E	F#	G#
5th ...	E	F#	G#	A	B	C#	D	E
3rd ...	C#	D	E	F#	G#	A	B	C#
Root...	A	B	C#	D	E	F#	G#	A
	$I^{\Delta 7}$	ii^7	iii^7	$IV^{\Delta 7}$	V^7	vi^7	$vii^{\o 7}$	$I^{\Delta 7}$

♫ A seventh chord is commonly voiced using just the root, third & seventh.

The Key of E Major

The E major scale uses the notes E, F♯, G♯, A, B, C♯, D♯ & E.

C Major ⁰ Sharps

G Major ¹ Sharp

D Major ² Sharps

A Major ³ Sharps

E Major ⁴ Sharps

B Major ⁵ Sharps
C♭ Enharmonic Equivalent

F♯ Major ⁶ Sharps
G♭ Enharmonic Equivalent

C♯ Major ⁷ Sharps
D♭ Enharmonic Equivalent

The Key of E Major

implies -- E, F♯, G♯, A, B, C♯ & D♯.

Signature

CLEFS & KEY SIGNATURE

Treble or G clef...

Alto or movable C clef...

Bass or F clef...

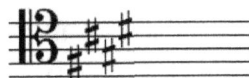

Tenor or movable C clef...

♪ The E major key signature has five sharps -- F♯, C♯, G♯ & D♯.

Progressions

COMMON PROGRESSIONS

I ⇨ *V* ⇨ *I* ...	implies	...	E Maj ⇨ B Maj ⇨ E Maj...
iii ⇨ *V* ⇨ *I* ...	implies	...	g♯ min ⇨ B Maj ⇨ E Maj...
I ⇨ *IV* ⇨ *V* ⇨ *I* ...	implies	...	E Maj ⇨ A Maj ⇨ B Maj ⇨ E Maj...
I ⇨ *ii* ⇨ *V* ⇨ *I* ...	implies	...	E Maj ⇨ f♯ min ⇨ B Maj ⇨ E Maj...
I ⇨ *vi* ⇨ *ii* ⇨ *V*...	implies	...	E Maj ⇨ c♯ min ⇨ f♯ min ⇨ B Maj...
iii ⇨ *vi* ⇨ *ii* ⇨ *V*...	implies	...	g♯ min ⇨ c♯ min ⇨ f♯ min ⇨ B Maj...

♪ The primary chords are E major [Tonic], A major [Subdominant] & B major [Dominant].

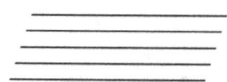

E Triads & Color Tones

The key of C# minor is...

Color Tones
DIATONIC CHORD STRUCTURE

6th	C#	D#	E	F#	G#	A	B	C#
4th	A	B	C#	D#	E	F#	G#	A
2nd	F#	G#	A	B	C#	D#	E	F#
5th ...	B	C#	D#	E	F#	G#	A	B
3rd ...	G#	A	B	C#	D#	E	F#	G#
Root...	E	F#	G#	A	B	C#	D#	E
	I	ii	iii	IV	V	vi	vii°	I

♫ Any color tone or tones may be voiced with the given triad chord.

Triads
DIATONIC CHORD STRUCTURE

5th ...	B	C#	D#	E	F#	G#	A	B
3rd ...	G#	A	B	C#	D#	E	F#	G#
Root...	E	F#	G#	A	B	C#	D#	E
	I	ii	iii	IV	V	vi	vii°	I

♫ A triad chord is commonly voiced using just the root & third.

E Sevenths & Extensions

...relative to the key of E major.

E x t e n s i o n s
DIATONIC CHORD STRUCTURE

13th	C#	D#	E	F#	G#	A	B	C#
11th	A	B	C#	D#	E	F#	G#	A
9th	F#	G#	A	B	C#	D#	E	F#
7th	D#	E	F#	G#	A	B	C#	D#
5th ...	B	C#	D#	E	F#	G#	A	B
3rd ...	G#	A	B	C#	D#	E	F#	G#
Root...	E	F#	G#	A	B	C#	D#	E
	$I^{\triangle 7}$	ii^7	iii^7	$IV^{\triangle 7}$	V^7	vi^7	$vii^{\emptyset 7}$	$I^{\triangle 7}$

♪ Any extension or extensions may be voiced with the given seventh chord.

S e v e n t h s
DIATONIC CHORD STRUCTURE

7th	D#	E	F#	G#	A	B	C#	D#
5th ...	B	C#	D#	E	F#	G#	A	B
3rd ...	G#	A	B	C#	D#	E	F#	G#
Root...	E	F#	G#	A	B	C#	D#	E
	$I^{\triangle 7}$	ii^7	iii^7	$IV^{\triangle 7}$	V^7	vi^7	$vii^{\emptyset 7}$	$I^{\triangle 7}$

♪ A seventh chord is commonly voiced using just the root, third & seventh.

C Major ^{0 Sharps}

G Major ^{1 Sharp}

D Major ^{2 Sharps}

A Major ^{3 Sharps}

E Major ^{4 Sharps}

B Major ^{5 Sharps}
C♭ Enharmonic Equivalent

F♯ Major ^{6 Sharps}
G♭ Enharmonic Equivalent

C♯ Major ^{7 Sharps}
D♭ Enharmonic Equivalent

The Key of B Major

The B major scale uses the notes B, C♯, D♯, E, F♯, G♯, A♯ & B.

The Key of B Major

implies -- B, C♯, D♯, E, F♯, G♯ & A♯.

Signature
CLEFS & KEY SIGNATURE

Treble or G clef...

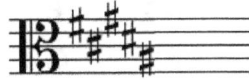

Alto or movable C clef...

Bass or F clef...

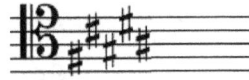

Tenor or movable C clef...

♪ The B major key signature has five sharps -- F♯, C♯, G♯, D♯, & A♯.

Progressions
COMMON PROGRESSIONS

I ⇨ V ⇨ I ...	implies ...	B Maj ⇨ F♯ Maj ⇨ B Maj...
iii ⇨ V ⇨ I ...	implies ...	d♯ min ⇨ F♯ Maj ⇨ B Maj...
I ⇨ IV ⇨ V ⇨ I ...	implies ...	B Maj ⇨ E Maj ⇨ F♯ Maj ⇨ B Maj...
I ⇨ ii ⇨ V ⇨ I ...	implies ...	B Maj ⇨ c♯ min ⇨ F♯ Maj ⇨ B Maj...
I ⇨ vi ⇨ ii ⇨ V...	implies ...	B Maj ⇨ g♯ min ⇨ c♯ min ⇨ F♯ Maj...
iii ⇨ vi ⇨ ii ⇨ V...	implies ...	d♯ min ⇨ g♯ min ⇨ c♯ min ⇨ F♯ Maj...

♪ The primary chords are B major ^Tonic^, E major ^Subdominant^ & F♯ major ^Dominant^.

B Triads & Color Tones

The key of G# minor is...

Color Tones
DIATONIC CHORD STRUCTURE

		I	ii	iii	IV	V	vi	vii°	I
6th		G#	A#	B	C#	D#	E	F#	G#
4th		E	F#	G#	A#	B	C#	D#	E
2nd		C#	D#	E	F#	G#	A#	B	C#
5th ...		F#	G#	A#	B	C#	D#	E	F#
3rd ...		D#	E	F#	G#	A#	B	C#	D#
Root...		B	C#	D#	E	F#	G#	A#	B
		I	*ii*	*iii*	*IV*	*V*	*vi*	*vii°*	*I*

♫ Any color tone or tones may be voiced with the given triad chord.

Triads
DIATONIC CHORD STRUCTURE

		I	ii	iii	IV	V	vi	vii°	I
5th ...		F#	G#	A#	B	C#	D#	E	F#
3rd ...		D#	E	F#	G#	A#	B	C#	D#
Root...		B	C#	D#	E	F#	G#	A#	B
		I	*ii*	*iii*	*IV*	*V*	*vi*	*vii°*	*I*

♫ A triad chord is commonly voiced using just the root & third.

B Sevenths & Extensions

...relative to the key of B major.

E x t e n s i o n s
DIATONIC CHORD STRUCTURE

13th	G#	A#	B	C#	D#	E	F#	G#
11th	E	F#	G#	A#	B	C#	D#	E
9th	C#	D#	E	F#	G#	A#	B	C#
7th	A#	B	C#	D#	E	F#	G#	A#
5th ...	F#	G#	A#	B	C#	D#	E	F#
3rd ...	D#	E	F#	G#	A#	B	C#	D#
Root...	B	C#	D#	E	F#	G#	A#	B
	$I^{\Delta 7}$	ii^7	iii^7	$IV^{\Delta 7}$	V^7	vi^7	$vii^{\varnothing 7}$	$I^{\Delta 7}$

♫ Any extension or extensions may be voiced with the given seventh chord.

S e v e n t h s
DIATONIC CHORD STRUCTURE

7th	A#	B	C#	D#	E	F#	G#	A#
5th ...	F#	G#	A#	B	C#	D#	E	F#
3rd ...	D#	E	F#	G#	A#	B	C#	D#
Root...	B	C#	D#	E	F#	G#	A#	B
	$I^{\Delta 7}$	ii^7	iii^7	$IV^{\Delta 7}$	V^7	vi^7	$vii^{\varnothing 7}$	$I^{\Delta 7}$

♫ A seventh chord is commonly voiced using just the root, third & seventh.

C Major ^{0 Sharps}

G Major ^{1 Sharp}

D Major ^{2 Sharps}

A Major ^{3 Sharps}

E Major ^{4 Sharps}

B Major ^{5 Sharps}
C♭ Enharmonic Equivalent

F# Major ^{6 Sharps}
G♭ Enharmonic Equivalent

C# Major ^{7 Sharps}
D♭ Enharmonic Equivalent

The Key of F# Major

The F# major scale uses the notes F#, G#, A#, B, C#, D#, E# & F#.

The Key of F♯ Major

implies -- F♯, G♯, A♯, B, C♯, D♯ & E♯.

Signature

CLEFS & KEY SIGNATURE

Treble or G clef...

Alto or movable C clef...

Bass or F clef...

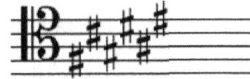

Tenor or movable C clef...

♪ The F♯ major key signature has six sharps -- F♯, C♯, G♯, D♯, A♯ & E♯.

Progressions

COMMON PROGRESSIONS

I ⇨ *V* ⇨ *I* ...	implies ...	F♯ Maj ⇨ C♯ Maj ⇨ F♯ Maj...
iii ⇨ *V* ⇨ *I* ...	implies ...	a♯ min ⇨ C♯ Maj ⇨ F♯ Maj...
I ⇨ *IV* ⇨ *V* ⇨ *I* ...	implies ...	F♯ Maj ⇨ B Maj ⇨ C♯ Maj ⇨ F♯ Maj...
I ⇨ *ii* ⇨ *V* ⇨ *I* ...	implies ...	F♯ Maj ⇨ g♯ min ⇨ C♯ Maj ⇨ F♯ Maj...
I ⇨ *vi* ⇨ *ii* ⇨ *V* ...	implies ...	F♯ Maj ⇨ d♯ min ⇨ g♯ min ⇨ C♯ Maj...
iii ⇨ *vi* ⇨ *ii* ⇨ *V* ...	implies ...	a♯ min ⇨ d♯ min ⇨ g♯ min ⇨ C♯ Maj...

♪ The primary chords are F♯ major ^Tonic, B major ^Subdominant & C♯ major ^Dominant.

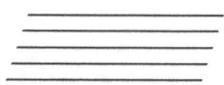

F# Triads & Color Tones

The key of D# minor is...

C o l o r   T o n e s

DIATONIC CHORD STRUCTURE

6th	D#	E#	F#	G#	A#	B	C#	A#
4th	B	C#	D#	E#	F#	G#	A#	B
2nd	G#	A#	B	C#	D#	E#	F#	G#
5th ...	C#	D#	E#	F#	G#	A#	B	C#
3rd ...	A#	B	C#	D#	E#	F#	G#	A#
Root...	F#	G#	A#	B	C#	D#	E#	F#
	I	*ii*	*iii*	*IV*	*V*	*vi*	*vii°*	*I*

♫ Any color tone or tones may be voiced with the given triad chord.

T r i a d s

DIATONIC CHORD STRUCTURE

5th ...	C#	D#	E#	F#	G#	A#	B	C#
3rd ...	A#	B	C#	D#	E#	F#	G#	A#
Root...	F#	G#	A#	B	C#	D#	E#	F#
	I	*ii*	*iii*	*IV*	*V*	*vi*	*vii°*	*I*

♫ A triad chord is commonly voiced using just the root & third.

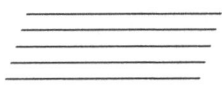

F# Sevenths & Extensions

...relative to the key of F# major.

Extensions
DIATONIC CHORD STRUCTURE

13th	D#	E#	F#	G#	A#	B	C#	D#
11th	B	C#	D#	E#	F#	G#	A#	B
9th	G#	A#	B	C#	D#	E#	F#	G#
7th	E#	F#	G#	A#	B	C#	D#	E#
5th ...	C#	D#	E#	F#	G#	A#	B	C#
3rd ...	A#	B	C#	D#	E#	F#	G#	A#
Root...	F#	G#	A#	B	C#	D#	E#	F#
	$I^{\triangle7}$	ii^{7}	iii^{7}	$IV^{\triangle7}$	V^{7}	vi^{7}	$vii^{\emptyset7}$	$I^{\triangle7}$

♫ Any extension or extensions may be voiced with the given seventh chord.

Sevenths
DIATONIC CHORD STRUCTURE

7th	E#	F#	G#	A#	B	C#	D#	E#
5th ...	C#	D#	E#	F#	G#	A#	B	C#
3rd ...	A#	B	C#	D#	E#	F#	G#	A#
Root...	F#	G#	A#	B	C#	D#	E#	F#
	$I^{\triangle7}$	ii^{7}	iii^{7}	$IV^{\triangle7}$	V^{7}	vi^{7}	$vii^{\emptyset7}$	$I^{\triangle7}$

♫ A seventh chord is commonly voiced using just the root, third & seventh.

C Major ^{0 Sharps}

G Major ^{1 Sharp}

D Major ^{2 Sharps}

A Major ^{3 Sharps}

E Major ^{4 Sharps}

B Major ^{5 Sharps}
Cb Enharmonic Equivalent

F# Major ^{6 Sharps}
Gb Enharmonic Equivalent

C# Major ^{7 Sharps}
Db Enharmonic Equivalent

The Key of C# Major

The C# major scale uses the notes C#, D#, E#, F#, G#, A#, B# & C#.

The Key of C♯ Major

implies -- C♯, D♯, E♯, F♯, G♯, A♯ & B♯.

Signature

CLEFS & KEY SIGNATURE

Treble or G clef...

Alto or movable C clef...

Bass or F clef...

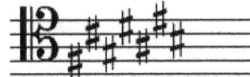

Tenor or movable C clef...

♪ The C♯ major key signature has seven sharps -- F♯, C♯, G♯, D♯, A♯, E♯ & B♯.

Progressions

COMMON PROGRESSIONS

I ⇨ V ⇨ I ...	implies	...	C♯ Maj ⇨ G♯ Maj ⇨ C♯ Maj...
iii ⇨ V ⇨ I ...	implies	...	e♯ min ⇨ G♯ Maj ⇨ C♯ Maj...
I ⇨ IV ⇨ V ⇨ I ...	implies	...	C♯ Maj ⇨ F♯ Maj ⇨ G♯ Maj ⇨ C♯ Maj...
I ⇨ ii ⇨ V ⇨ I ...	implies	...	C♯ Maj ⇨ d♯ min ⇨ G♯ Maj ⇨ C♯ Maj...
I ⇨ vi ⇨ ii ⇨ V ...	implies	...	C♯ Maj ⇨ a♯ min ⇨ d♯ min ⇨ G♯ Maj...
iii ⇨ vi ⇨ ii ⇨ V ...	implies	...	e♯ min ⇨ a♯ min ⇨ d♯ min ⇨ G♯ Maj...

♪ The primary chords are C♯ major [Tonic], F♯ major [Subdominant] & G♯ major [Dominant].

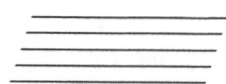

C# Triads & Color Tones

The key of A# minor is...

Color Tones

DIATONIC CHORD STRUCTURE

6th	A#	B#	C#	D#	E#	F#	G#	A#
4th	F#	G#	A#	B#	C#	D#	E#	F#
2nd	D#	E#	F#	G#	A#	B#	C#	D#
5th ...	G#	A#	B#	C#	D#	E#	F#	G#
3rd ...	E#	F#	G#	A#	B#	C#	D#	E#
Root...	C#	D#	E#	F#	G#	A#	B#	C#
	I	*ii*	*iii*	*IV*	*V*	*vi*	*vii°*	*I*

♪ Any color tone or tones may be voiced with the given triad chord.

Triads

DIATONIC CHORD STRUCTURE

5th ...	G#	A#	B#	C#	D#	E#	F#	G#
3rd ...	E#	F#	G#	A#	B#	C#	D#	E#
Root...	C#	D#	E#	F#	G#	A#	B#	C#
	I	*ii*	*iii*	*IV*	*V*	*vi*	*vii°*	*I*

♪ A triad chord is commonly voiced using just the root & third.

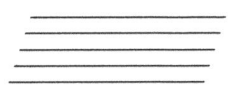

C# Sevenths & Extensions

...relative to the key of C# major.

Extensions
DIATONIC CHORD STRUCTURE

13th	A#	B#	C#	D#	E#	F#	G#	A#
11th	F#	G#	A#	B#	C#	D#	E#	F#
9th	D#	E#	F#	G#	A#	B#	C#	D#
7th	B#	C#	D#	E#	F#	G#	A#	B#
5th ...	G#	A#	B#	C#	D#	E#	F#	G#
3rd ...	E#	F#	G#	A#	B#	C#	D#	E#
Root...	C#	D#	E#	F#	G#	A#	B#	C#
	$I^{\triangle 7}$	ii^7	iii^7	$IV^{\triangle 7}$	V^7	vi^7	$vii^{\varnothing 7}$	$I^{\triangle 7}$

♫ Any extension or extensions may be voiced with the given seventh chord.

Sevenths
DIATONIC CHORD STRUCTURE

7th	B#	C#	D#	E#	F#	G#	A#	B#
5th ...	G#	A#	B#	C#	D#	E#	F#	G#
3rd ...	E#	F#	G#	A#	B#	C#	D#	E#
Root...	C#	D#	E#	F#	G#	A#	B#	C#
	$I^{\triangle 7}$	ii^7	iii^7	$IV^{\triangle 7}$	V^7	vi^7	$vii^{\varnothing 7}$	$I^{\triangle 7}$

♫ A seventh chord is commonly voiced using just the root, third & seventh.

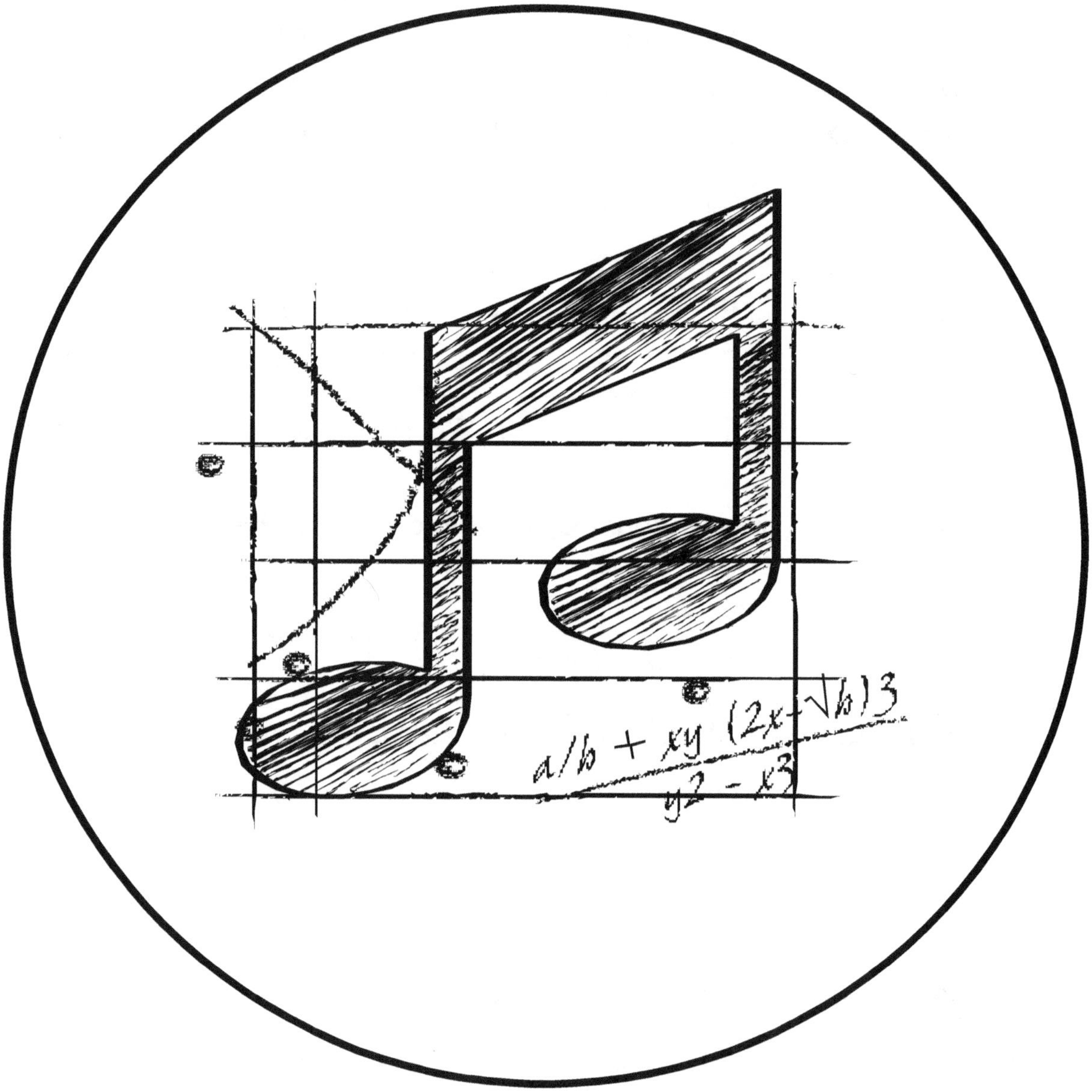
a/b + xy (2x-√b)3
y2 - x3

b

CHAPTER TWO

The Flat Major Keys

C♭ Major 7 Flats
B Enharmonic Equivalent

G♭ Major 6 Flats
F♯ Enharmonic Equivalent

D♭ Major 5 Flats
C♯ Enharmonic Equivalent

A♭ Major 4 Flats

E♭ Major 3 Flats

B♭ Major 2 Flats

F Major 1 Flat

C Major 0 Flats

The Key of C♭ Major

The C♭ major scale uses the notes C♭, D♭, E♭, F♭, G♭, A♭, B♭ & C♭.

The Key of C♭ Major
implies -- C♭, D♭, E♭, F♭, G♭, A♭ & B♭.

Signature
CLEFS & KEY SIGNATURE

Treble or G clef...

Alto or movable C clef...

Bass or F clef...

Tenor or moveable C clef...

♫ The C♭ major signature has seven flats -- B♭, E♭, A♭, D♭, G♭, C♭ & F♭.

Progressions
COMMON PROGRESSIONS

I ⇒ V ⇒ I ...	implies ...	C♭ Maj ⇒ G♭ Maj ⇒ C♭ Maj...
iii ⇒ V ⇒ I ...	implies ...	e♭ min ⇒ G♭ Maj ⇒ C♭ Maj...
I ⇒ IV ⇒ V ⇒ I ...	implies ...	C♭ Maj ⇒ F♭ Maj ⇒ G♭ Maj ⇒ C♭ Maj...
I ⇒ ii ⇒ V ⇒ I ...	implies ...	C♭ Maj ⇒ d♭ min ⇒ G♭ Maj ⇒ C♭ Maj...
I ⇒ vi ⇒ ii ⇒ V...	implies ...	C♭ Maj ⇒ a♭ min ⇒ d♭ min ⇒ G♭ Maj...
iii ⇒ vi ⇒ ii ⇒ V...	implies ...	e♭ min ⇒ a♭ min ⇒ d♭ min ⇒ G♭ Maj...

♫ The primary chords are C♭ major ᵀᵒⁿⁱᶜ, F♭ major ˢᵘᵇᵈᵒᵐⁱⁿᵃⁿᵗ & G♭ major ᴰᵒᵐⁱⁿᵃⁿᵗ.

C♭ Triads & Color Tones

The key of A♭ minor is...

Color Tones

DIATONIC CHORD STRUCTURE

6th	A♭	B♭	C♭	D♭	E♭	F♭	G♭	A♭
4th	F♭	G♭	A♭	B♭	C♭	D♭	E♭	F♭
2nd	D♭	E♭	F♭	G♭	A♭	B♭	C♭	D♭
5th ...	G♭	A♭	B♭	C♭	D♭	E♭	F♭	G♭
3rd ...	E♭	F♭	G♭	A♭	B♭	C♭	D♭	E♭
Root...	C♭	D♭	E♭	F♭	G♭	A♭	B♭	C♭
	I	ii	iii	IV	V	vi	vii°	I

♫ Any color tone or tones may be voiced with the given triad chord.

Triads

DIATONIC CHORD STRUCTURE

5th ...	G♭	A♭	B♭	C♭	D♭	E♭	F♭	G♭
3rd ...	E♭	F♭	G♭	A♭	B♭	C♭	D♭	E♭
Root...	C♭	D♭	E♭	F♭	G♭	A♭	B♭	C♭
	I	ii	iii	IV	V	vi	vii°	I

♫ A triad chord is commonly voiced using just the root & third.

Cb Sevenths & Extensions

...relative to the key of Cb major.

Extensions
DIATONIC CHORD STRUCTURE

13th	Ab	Bb	Cb	Db	Eb	Fb	Gb	Ab
11th	Fb	Gb	Ab	Bb	Cb	Db	Eb	Fb
9th	Db	Eb	Fb	Gb	Ab	Bb	Cb	Db
7th	Bb	Cb	Db	Eb	Fb	Gb	Ab	Bb
5th ...	Gb	Ab	Bb	Cb	Db	Eb	Fb	Gb
3rd ...	Eb	Fb	Gb	Ab	Bb	Cb	Db	Eb
Root...	Cb	Db	Eb	Fb	Gb	Ab	Bb	Cb
	$I^{\triangle 7}$	ii^{7}	iii^{7}	$IV^{\triangle 7}$	V^{7}	vi^{7}	$vii^{\varnothing 7}$	$I^{\triangle 7}$

♪ Any extension or extensions may be voiced with the given seventh chord.

Sevenths
DIATONIC CHORD STRUCTURE

7th	Bb	Cb	Db	Eb	Fb	Gb	Ab	Bb
5th ...	Gb	Ab	Bb	Cb	Db	Eb	Fb	Gb
3rd ...	Eb	Fb	Gb	Ab	Bb	Cb	Db	Eb
Root...	Cb	Db	Eb	Fb	Gb	Ab	Bb	Cb
	$I^{\triangle 7}$	ii^{7}	iii^{7}	$IV^{\triangle 7}$	V^{7}	vi^{7}	$vii^{\varnothing 7}$	$I^{\triangle 7}$

♪ A seventh chord is commonly voiced using just the root, third & seventh.

C♭ Major ⁷ Flats

B Enharmonic Equivalent

G♭ Major ⁶ Flats

F♯ Enharmonic Equivalent

D♭ Major ⁵ Flats

C♯ Enharmonic Equivalent

A♭ Major ⁴ Flats

E♭ Major ³ Flats

B♭ Major ² Flats

F Major ¹ Flat

C Major ⁰ Flats

The Key of G♭ Major

The G♭ major scale uses the notes G♭, A♭, B♭, C♭, D♭ E♭, F & G♭.

The Key of G♭ Major

implies -- G♭, A♭, B♭, C♭, D♭, E♭ & F.

Signature

CLEFS & KEY SIGNATURE

Treble or G clef...

Alto or movable C clef...

Bass or F clef...

Tenor or moveable C clef...

♪ The G♭ major signature has six flats -- B♭, E♭, A♭, D♭, G♭ & C♭.

Progressions

COMMON PROGRESSIONS

I ⇒ V ⇒ I ...	implies	...	G♭ Maj ⇒ D♭ Maj ⇒ G♭ Maj...
iii ⇒ V ⇒ I ...	implies	...	b♭ min ⇒ D♭ Maj ⇒ G♭ Maj...
I ⇒ IV ⇒ V ⇒ I ...	implies	...	G♭ Maj ⇒ C♭ Maj ⇒ D♭ Maj ⇒ G♭ Maj...
I ⇒ ii ⇒ V ⇒ I ...	implies	...	G♭ Maj ⇒ a♭ min ⇒ D♭ Maj ⇒ G♭ Maj...
I ⇒ vi ⇒ ii ⇒ V ...	implies	...	G♭ Maj ⇒ e♭ min ⇒ a♭ min ⇒ D♭ Maj...
iii ⇒ vi ⇒ ii ⇒ V ...	implies	...	b♭ min ⇒ e♭ min ⇒ a♭ min ⇒ D♭ Maj...

♪ The primary chords are G♭ major ᵀᵒⁿⁱᶜ, C♭ major ˢᵘᵇᵈᵒᵐⁱⁿᵃⁿᵗ & D♭ major ᴰᵒᵐⁱⁿᵃⁿᵗ.

G♭ Triads & Color Tones

The key of E♭ minor is...

Color Tones

DIATONIC CHORD STRUCTURE

6th	E♭	F	G♭	A♭	B♭	C♭	D♭	E♭
4th	C♭	D♭	E♭	F	G♭	A♭	B♭	C♭
2nd	A♭	B♭	C♭	D♭	E♭	F	G♭	A♭
5th ...	D♭	E♭	F	G♭	A♭	B♭	C♭	D♭
3rd ...	B♭	C♭	D♭	E♭	F	G♭	A♭	B♭
Root...	G♭	A♭	B♭	C♭	D♭	E♭	F	G♭
	I	ii	iii	IV	V	vi	vii°	I

♪ Any color tone or tones may be voiced with the given triad chord.

Triads

DIATONIC CHORD STRUCTURE

5th ...	D♭	E♭	F	G♭	A♭	B♭	C♭	D♭
3rd ...	B♭	C♭	D♭	E♭	F	G♭	A♭	B♭
Root...	G♭	A♭	B♭	C♭	D♭	E♭	F	G♭
	I	ii	iii	IV	V	vi	vii°	I

♪ A triad chord is commonly voiced using just the root & third.

G♭ Sevenths & Extensions

...relative to the key of G♭ major.

Extensions
DIATONIC CHORD STRUCTURE

13th	E♭	F	G♭	A♭	B♭	C♭	D♭	E♭
11th	C♭	D♭	E♭	F	G♭	A♭	B♭	C♭
9th	A♭	B♭	C♭	D♭	E♭	F	G♭	A♭
7th	F	G♭	A♭	B♭	C♭	D♭	E♭	F
5th ...	D♭	E♭	F	G♭	A♭	B♭	C♭	D♭
3rd ...	B♭	C♭	D♭	E♭	F	G♭	A♭	B♭
Root...	G♭	A♭	B♭	C♭	D♭	E♭	F	G♭
	$I^{\triangle 7}$	ii^7	iii^7	$IV^{\triangle 7}$	V^7	vi^7	$vii^{\varnothing 7}$	$I^{\triangle 7}$

♫ Any extension or extensions may be voiced with the given seventh chord.

Sevenths
DIATONIC CHORD STRUCTURE

7th	F	G♭	A♭	B♭	C♭	D♭	E♭	F
5th ...	D♭	E♭	F	G♭	A♭	B♭	C♭	D♭
3rd ...	B♭	C♭	D♭	E♭	F	G♭	A♭	B♭
Root...	G♭	A♭	B♭	C♭	D♭	E♭	F	G♭
	$I^{\triangle 7}$	ii^7	iii^7	$IV^{\triangle 7}$	V^7	vi^7	$vii^{\varnothing 7}$	$I^{\triangle 7}$

♫ A seventh chord is commonly voiced using just the root, third & seventh.

C♭ Major ⁷ ᶠˡᵃᵗˢ

B Enharmonic Equivalent

G♭ Major ⁶ ᶠˡᵃᵗˢ

F♯ Enharmonic Equivalent

D♭ Major ⁵ ᶠˡᵃᵗˢ

C♯ Enharmonic Equivalent

A♭ Major ⁴ ᶠˡᵃᵗˢ

E♭ Major ³ ᶠˡᵃᵗˢ

B♭ Major ² ᶠˡᵃᵗˢ

F Major ¹ ᶠˡᵃᵗ

C Major ⁰ ᶠˡᵃᵗˢ

The Key of D♭ Major

The D♭ major scale uses the notes D♭, E♭, F, G♭, A♭, B♭, C & D♭.

The Key of D♭ Major

implies -- D♭, E♭, F, G♭, A♭, B♭ & C.

Signature

CLEFS & KEY SIGNATURE

Treble or G clef...

Alto or movable C clef...

Bass or F clef...

Tenor or moveable C clef...

♫ The D♭ major signature has five flats -- B♭, E♭, A♭, D♭ & G♭.

Progressions

COMMON PROGRESSIONS

I ⇨ V ⇨ I ...	implies	...	D♭ Maj ⇨ A♭ Maj ⇨ D♭ Maj...
iii ⇨ V ⇨ I ...	implies	...	f min ⇨ A♭ Maj ⇨ D♭ Maj...
I ⇨ IV ⇨ V ⇨ I ...	implies	...	D♭ Maj ⇨ G♭ Maj ⇨ A♭ Maj ⇨ D♭ Maj...
I ⇨ ii ⇨ V ⇨ I ...	implies	...	D♭ Maj ⇨ e♭ min ⇨ A♭ Maj ⇨ D♭ Maj...
I ⇨ vi ⇨ ii ⇨ V ...	implies	...	D♭ Maj ⇨ b♭ min ⇨ e♭ min ⇨ A♭ Maj...
iii ⇨ vi ⇨ ii ⇨ V ...	implies	...	f min ⇨ b♭ min ⇨ e♭ min ⇨ A♭ Maj...

♫ The primary chords are D♭ major ᵀᵒⁿⁱᶜ, G♭ major ˢᵘᵇᵈᵒᵐⁱⁿᵃⁿᵗ & A♭ major ᴰᵒᵐⁱⁿᵃⁿᵗ.

D♭ Triads & Color Tones

The key of B♭ minor is...

Color Tones

DIATONIC CHORD STRUCTURE

6th	B♭	C	D♭	E♭	F	G♭	A♭	B♭
4th	G♭	A♭	B♭	C	D♭	E♭	F	G♭
2nd	E♭	F	G♭	A♭	B♭	C	D♭	E♭
5th ...	A♭	B♭	C	D♭	E♭	F	G♭	A♭
3rd ...	F	G♭	A♭	B♭	C	D♭	E♭	F
Root...	D♭	E♭	F	G♭	A♭	B♭	C	D♭
	I	ii	iii	IV	V	vi	vii°	I

♫ Any color tone or tones may be voiced with the given triad chord.

Triads

DIATONIC CHORD STRUCTURE

5th ...	A♭	B♭	C	D♭	E♭	F	G♭	A♭
3rd ...	F	G♭	A♭	B♭	C	D♭	E♭	F
Root...	D♭	E♭	F	G♭	A♭	B♭	C	D♭
	I	ii	iii	IV	V	vi	vii°	I

♫ A triad chord is commonly voiced using just the root & third.

D♭ Sevenths & Extensions

...relative to the key of D♭ major.

Extensions

DIATONIC CHORD STRUCTURE

13th	B♭	C	D♭	E♭	F	G♭	A♭	B♭
11th	G♭	A♭	B♭	C	D♭	E♭	F	G♭
9th	E♭	F	G♭	A♭	B♭	C	D♭	E♭
7th	C	D♭	E♭	F	G♭	A♭	B♭	C
5th ...	A♭	B♭	C	D♭	E♭	F	G♭	A♭
3rd ...	F	G♭	A♭	B♭	C	D♭	E♭	F
Root...	D♭	E♭	F	G♭	A♭	B♭	C	D♭
	$I^{\triangle 7}$	ii^{7}	iii^{7}	$IV^{\triangle 7}$	V^{7}	vi^{7}	$vii^{\emptyset 7}$	$I^{\triangle 7}$

♫ Any extension or extensions may be voiced with the given seventh chord.

Sevenths

DIATONIC CHORD STRUCTURE

7th	C	D♭	E♭	F	G♭	A♭	B♭	C
5th ...	A♭	B♭	C	D♭	E♭	F	G♭	A♭
3rd ...	F	G♭	A♭	B♭	C	D♭	E♭	F
Root...	D♭	E♭	F	G♭	A♭	B♭	C	D♭
	$I^{\triangle 7}$	ii^{7}	iii^{7}	$IV^{\triangle 7}$	V^{7}	vi^{7}	$vii^{\emptyset 7}$	$I^{\triangle 7}$

♫ A seventh chord is commonly voiced using just the root, third & seventh.

UNABRIDGED DIATONICS™   A COMPLETE DIATONIC REFERENCE – THE CIRCLE OF FIFTHS

Cb Major ^{7 Flats}

B Enharmonic Equivalent

Gb Major ^{6 Flats}

F♯ Enharmonic Equivalent

Db Major ^{5 Flats}

C♯ Enharmonic Equivalent

Ab Major ^{4 Flats}

Eb Major ^{3 Flats}

Bb Major ^{2 Flats}

F Major ^{1 Flat}

C Major ^{0 Flats}

The Key of Ab Major

The Ab major scale uses the notes Ab, Bb, C, Db, Eb F, G & Ab.

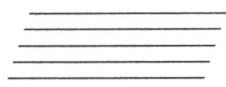

The Key of A♭ Major

implies -- A♭, B♭, C, D♭, E♭, F & G.

Signature

CLEFS & KEY SIGNATURE

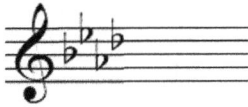

Treble or G clef...

Alto or movable C clef...

Bass or F clef...

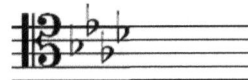

Tenor or moveable C clef...

♫ The A♭ major signature has four flats -- B♭, E♭, A♭ & D♭.

Progressions

COMMON PROGRESSIONS

I ⇨ V ⇨ I ...	implies	...	A♭ Maj ⇨ E♭ Maj ⇨ A♭ Maj...
iii ⇨ V ⇨ I ...	implies	...	c min ⇨ E♭ Maj ⇨ A♭ Maj...
I ⇨ IV ⇨ V ⇨ I ...	implies	...	A♭ Maj ⇨ D♭ Maj ⇨ E♭ Maj ⇨ A♭ Maj...
I ⇨ ii ⇨ V ⇨ I ...	implies	...	A♭ Maj ⇨ b♭ min ⇨ E♭ Maj ⇨ A♭ Maj...
I ⇨ vi ⇨ ii ⇨ V...	implies	...	A♭ Maj ⇨ f min ⇨ b♭ min ⇨ E♭ Maj...
iii ⇨ vi ⇨ ii ⇨ V...	implies	...	c min ⇨ f min ⇨ b♭ min ⇨ E♭ Maj...

♫ The primary chords are A♭ major ^Tonic, D♭ major ^Subdominant & E♭ major ^Dominant.

A♭ Triads & Color Tones

The key of F minor is...

Color Tones

DIATONIC CHORD STRUCTURE

6th	F	G	A♭	B♭	C	D♭	E♭	F
4th	D♭	E♭	F	G	A♭	B♭	C	D♭
2nd	B♭	C	D♭	E♭	F	G	A♭	B♭
5th ...	E♭	F	G	A♭	B♭	C	D♭	E♭
3rd ...	C	D♭	E♭	F	G	A♭	B♭	C
Root...	A♭	B♭	C	D♭	E♭	F	G	A♭
	I	ii	iii	IV	V	vi	vii°	I

♪ Any color tone or tones may be voiced with the given triad chord.

Triads

DIATONIC CHORD STRUCTURE

5th ...	E♭	F	G	A♭	B♭	C	D♭	E♭
3rd ...	C	D♭	E♭	F	G	A♭	B♭	C
Root...	A♭	B♭	C	D♭	E♭	F	G	A♭
	I	ii	iii	IV	V	vi	vii°	I

♪ A triad chord is commonly voiced using just the root & third.

A♭ Sevenths & Extensions

...relative to the key of A♭ major.

Extensions
DIATONIC CHORD STRUCTURE

13th	F	G	A♭	B♭	C	D♭	E♭	F
11th	D♭	E♭	F	G	A♭	B♭	C	D♭
9th	B♭	C	D♭	E♭	F	G	A♭	B♭
7th	G	A♭	B♭	C	D♭	E♭	F	G
5th ...	E♭	F	G	A♭	B♭	C	D♭	E♭
3rd ...	C	D♭	E♭	F	G	A♭	B♭	C
Root...	A♭	B♭	C	D♭	E♭	F	G	A♭
	$I^{\triangle 7}$	ii^7	iii^7	$IV^{\triangle 7}$	V^7	vi^7	$vii^{\varnothing 7}$	$I^{\triangle 7}$

♫ Any extension or extensions may be voiced with the given seventh chord.

Sevenths
DIATONIC CHORD STRUCTURE

7th	G	A♭	B♭	C	D♭	E♭	F	G
5th ...	E♭	F	G	A♭	B♭	C	D♭	E♭
3rd ...	C	D♭	E♭	F	G	A♭	B♭	C
Root...	A♭	B♭	C	D♭	E♭	F	G	A♭
	$I^{\triangle 7}$	ii^7	iii^7	$IV^{\triangle 7}$	V^7	vi^7	$vii^{\varnothing 7}$	$I^{\triangle 7}$

♫ A seventh chord is commonly voiced using just the root, third & seventh.

Cb Major ⁷ Flats

B Enharmonic Equivalent

Gb Major ⁶ Flats

F# Enharmonic Equivalent

Db Major ⁵ Flats

C# Enharmonic Equivalent

Ab Major ⁴ Flats

Eb Major ³ Flats

Bb Major ² Flats

F Major ¹ Flat

C Major ⁰ Flats

The Key of Eb Major

The Eb major scale uses the notes Eb, F, G, Ab, Bb, C, D & Eb.

The Key of E♭ Major

implies -- E♭, F, G, A♭, B♭, C & D.

Signature

CLEFS & KEY SIGNATURE

Treble or G clef...

Alto or movable C clef...

Bass or F clef...

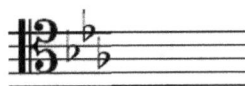

Tenor or moveable C clef...

♪ The E♭ major signature has three flats -- B♭, E♭ & A♭.

Progressions

COMMON PROGRESSIONS

I ⇨ V ⇨ I ...	implies ...	E♭ Maj ⇨ B♭ Maj ⇨ E♭ Maj...
iii ⇨ V ⇨ I ...	implies ...	g min ⇨ B♭ Maj ⇨ E♭ Maj...
I ⇨ IV ⇨ V ⇨ I ...	implies ...	E♭ Maj ⇨ A♭ Maj ⇨ B♭ Maj ⇨ E♭ Maj...
I ⇨ ii ⇨ V ⇨ I ...	implies ...	E♭ Maj ⇨ f min ⇨ B♭ Maj ⇨ E♭ Maj...
I ⇨ vi ⇨ ii ⇨ V ...	implies ...	E♭ Maj ⇨ c min ⇨ f min ⇨ B♭ Maj...
iii ⇨ vi ⇨ ii ⇨ V ...	implies ...	g min ⇨ c min ⇨ f min ⇨ B♭ Maj...

♪ The primary chords are E♭ major ^Tonic, A♭ major ^Subdominant & B♭ major ^Dominant.

Eb Triads & Color Tones

The key of C minor is...

Color Tones

DIATONIC CHORD STRUCTURE

6th	C	D	Eb	F	G	Ab	Bb	C
4th	Ab	Bb	C	D	Eb	F	G	Ab
2nd	F	G	Ab	Bb	C	D	Eb	F
5th ...	Bb	C	D	Eb	F	G	Ab	Bb
3rd ...	G	Ab	Bb	C	D	Eb	F	G
Root...	Eb	F	G	Ab	Bb	C	D	Eb
	I	ii	iii	IV	V	vi	vii°	I

♫ Any color tone or tones may be voiced with the given triad chord.

Triads

DIATONIC CHORD STRUCTURE

5th ...	Bb	C	D	Eb	F	G	Ab	Bb
3rd ...	G	Ab	Bb	C	D	Eb	F	G
Root...	Eb	F	G	Ab	Bb	C	D	Eb
	I	ii	iii	IV	V	vi	vii°	I

♫ A triad chord is commonly voiced using just the root & third.

Eb Sevenths & Extensions

...relative to the key of Eb major.

Extensions
DIATONIC CHORD STRUCTURE

13th	C	D	Eb	F	G	Ab	Bb	C
11th	Ab	Bb	C	D	Eb	F	G	Ab
9th	F	G	Ab	Bb	C	D	Eb	F
7th	D	Eb	F	G	Ab	Bb	C	D
5th ...	Bb	C	D	Eb	F	G	Ab	Bb
3rd ...	G	Ab	Bb	C	D	Eb	F	G
Root...	Eb	F	G	Ab	Bb	C	D	Eb
	$I^{\triangle 7}$	ii^{7}	iii^{7}	$IV^{\triangle 7}$	V^{7}	vi^{7}	$vii^{\varnothing 7}$	$I^{\triangle 7}$

♪ Any extension or extensions may be voiced with the given seventh chord.

Sevenths
DIATONIC CHORD STRUCTURE

7th	D	Eb	F	G	Ab	Bb	C	D
5th ...	Bb	C	D	Eb	F	G	Ab	Bb
3rd ...	G	Ab	Bb	C	D	Eb	F	G
Root...	Eb	F	G	Ab	Bb	C	D	Eb
	$I^{\triangle 7}$	ii^{7}	iii^{7}	$IV^{\triangle 7}$	V^{7}	vi^{7}	$vii^{\varnothing 7}$	$I^{\triangle 7}$

♪ A seventh chord is commonly voiced using just the root, third & seventh.

Cb Major ⁷ Flats
B Enharmonic Equivalent

Gb Major ⁶ Flats
F# Enharmonic Equivalent

Db Major ⁵ Flats
C# Enharmonic Equivalent

Ab Major ⁴ Flats

Eb Major ³ Flats

Bb Major ² Flats

F Major ¹ Flat

C Major ⁰ Flats

The Key of Bb Major

The Bb major scale uses the notes Bb, C, D, Eb, F, G, A & Bb.

The Key of B♭ Major

implies -- B♭, C, D, E♭, F, G & A.

Signature

CLEFS & KEY SIGNATURE

Treble or G clef...

Alto or movable C clef...

Bass or F clef...

Tenor or moveable C clef...

♫ The B♭ major signature has two flats -- B♭ & E♭.

Progressions

COMMON PROGRESSIONS

I ⇨ V ⇨ I ...	implies ...	B♭ Maj ⇨ F Maj ⇨ B♭ Maj...
iii ⇨ V ⇨ I ...	implies ...	d min ⇨ F Maj ⇨ B♭ Maj...
I ⇨ IV ⇨ V ⇨ I ...	implies ...	B♭ Maj ⇨ E♭ Maj ⇨ F Maj ⇨ B♭ Maj...
I ⇨ ii ⇨ V ⇨ I ...	implies ...	B♭ Maj ⇨ c min ⇨ F Maj ⇨ B♭ Maj...
I ⇨ vi ⇨ ii ⇨ V ...	implies ...	B♭ Maj ⇨ g min ⇨ c min ⇨ F Maj...
iii ⇨ vi ⇨ ii ⇨ V ...	implies ...	d min ⇨ g min ⇨ c min ⇨ F Maj...

♫ The primary chords are B♭ major ᵀᵒⁿⁱᶜ, E♭ major ˢᵘᵇᵈᵒᵐⁱⁿᵃⁿᵗ & F major ᴰᵒᵐⁱⁿᵃⁿᵗ.

B♭ Triads & Color Tones

The key of G minor is...

Color Tones

DIATONIC CHORD STRUCTURE

6th	G	A	B♭	C	D	E♭	F	G
4th	E♭	F	G	A	B♭	C	D	E♭
2nd	C	D	E♭	F	G	A	B♭	C
5th ...	F	G	A	B♭	C	D	E♭	F
3rd ...	D	E♭	F	G	A	B♭	C	D
Root...	B♭	C	D	E♭	F	G	A	B♭
	I	ii	iii	IV	V	vi	vii°	I

♪ Any color tone or tones may be voiced with the given triad chord.

Triads

DIATONIC CHORD STRUCTURE

5th ...	F	G	A	B♭	C	D	E♭	F
3rd ...	D	E♭	F	G	A	B♭	C	D
Root...	B♭	C	D	E♭	F	G	A	B♭
	I	ii	iii	IV	V	vi	vii°	I

♪ A triad chord is commonly voiced using just the root & third.

B♭ Sevenths & Extensions

...relative to the key of B♭ major.

E x t e n s i o n s
DIATONIC CHORD STRUCTURE

13th	G	A	B♭	C	D	E♭	F	G
11th	E♭	F	G	A	B♭	C	D	E♭
9th	C	D	E♭	F	G	A	B♭	C
7th	A	B♭	C	D	E♭	F	G	A
5th ...	F	G	A	B♭	C	D	E♭	F
3rd ...	D	E♭	F	G	A	B♭	C	D
Root...	B♭	C	D	E♭	F	G	A	B♭
	$I^{\triangle 7}$	ii^{7}	iii^{7}	$IV^{\triangle 7}$	V^{7}	vi^{7}	$vii^{\emptyset 7}$	$I^{\triangle 7}$

♪ Any extension or extensions may be voiced with the given seventh chord.

S e v e n t h s
DIATONIC CHORD STRUCTURE

7th	A	B♭	C	D	E♭	F	G	A
5th ...	F	G	A	B♭	C	D	E♭	F
3rd ...	D	E♭	F	G	A	B♭	C	D
Root...	B♭	C	D	E♭	F	G	A	B♭
	$I^{\triangle 7}$	ii^{7}	iii^{7}	$IV^{\triangle 7}$	V^{7}	vi^{7}	$vii^{\emptyset 7}$	$I^{\triangle 7}$

♪ A seventh chord is commonly voiced using just the root, third & seventh.

Cb Major ^{7 Flats}

B Enharmonic Equivalent

Gb Major ^{6 Flats}

F# Enharmonic Equivalent

Db Major ^{5 Flats}

C# Enharmonic Equivalent

Ab Major ^{4 Flats}

Eb Major ^{3 Flats}

Bb Major ^{2 Flats}

F Major ^{1 Flat}

C Major ^{0 Flats}

The Key of F Major

The F major scale uses the notes F, G, A, Bb, C, D, E & F.

The Key of F Major

implies -- F, G, A, Bb, C, D & E.

Signature

CLEFS & KEY SIGNATURE

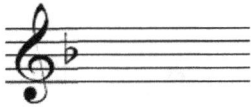

Treble or G clef...

Alto or movable C clef...

Bass or F clef...

Tenor or moveable C clef...

♫ The F major signature has one flat – Bb.

Progressions

COMMON PROGRESSIONS

I ⇨ V ⇨ I ...	implies	...	F Maj ⇨ C Maj ⇨ F Maj...
iii ⇨ V ⇨ I ...	implies	...	a min ⇨ C Maj ⇨ F Maj...
I ⇨ IV ⇨ V ⇨ I ...	implies	...	F Maj ⇨ Bb Maj ⇨ C Maj ⇨ F Maj...
I ⇨ ii ⇨ V ⇨ I ...	implies	...	F Maj ⇨ g min ⇨ C Maj ⇨ F Maj...
I ⇨ vi ⇨ ii ⇨ V ...	implies	...	F Maj ⇨ d min ⇨ g min ⇨ C Maj...
iii ⇨ vi ⇨ ii ⇨ V ...	implies	...	a min ⇨ d min ⇨ g min ⇨ C Maj...

♫ The primary chords are F major ^{Tonic}, Bb major ^{Subdominant} & C major ^{Dominant}.

F Triads & Color Tones

The key of D minor is...

Color Tones
DIATONIC CHORD STRUCTURE

	I	ii	iii	IV	V	vi	vii°	I
6th	D	E	F	G	A	B♭	C	D
4th	B♭	C	D	E	F	G	A	B♭
2nd	G	A	B♭	C	D	E	F	G
5th ...	C	D	E	F	G	A	B♭	C
3rd ...	A	B♭	C	D	E	F	G	A
Root...	F	G	A	B♭	C	D	E	F

♪ Any color tone or tones may be voiced with the given triad chord.

Triads
DIATONIC CHORD STRUCTURE

	I	ii	iii	IV	V	vi	vii°	I
5th ...	C	D	E	F	G	A	B♭	C
3rd ...	A	B♭	C	D	E	F	G	A
Root...	F	G	A	B♭	C	D	E	F

♪ A triad chord is commonly voiced using just the root & third.

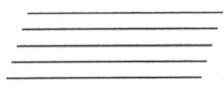

F Sevenths & Extensions

...relative to the key of F major.

E x t e n s i o n s
DIATONIC CHORD STRUCTURE

13th	D	E	F	G	A	Bb	C	D
11th	Bb	C	D	E	F	G	A	Bb
9th	G	A	Bb	C	D	E	F	G
7th	E	F	G	A	Bb	C	D	E
5th ...	C	D	E	F	G	A	Bb	C
3rd ...	A	Bb	C	D	E	F	G	A
Root...	F	G	A	Bb	C	D	E	F
	$I^{\triangle 7}$	ii^7	iii^7	$IV^{\triangle 7}$	V^7	vi^7	$vii^{\o 7}$	$I^{\triangle 7}$

♫ Any extension or extensions may be voiced with the given seventh chord.

S e v e n t h s
DIATONIC CHORD STRUCTURE

7th	E	F	G	A	Bb	C	D	E
5th ...	C	D	E	F	G	A	Bb	C
3rd ...	A	Bb	C	D	E	F	G	A
Root...	F	G	A	Bb	C	D	E	F
	$I^{\triangle 7}$	ii^7	iii^7	$IV^{\triangle 7}$	V^7	vi^7	$vii^{\o 7}$	$I^{\triangle 7}$

♫ A seventh chord is commonly voiced using just the root, third & seventh.

Cb Major ⁷ Flats
B Enharmonic Equivalent

Gb Major ⁶ Flats
F♯ Enharmonic Equivalent

Db Major ⁵ Flats
C♯ Enharmonic Equivalent

Ab Major ⁴ Flats

Eb Major ³ Flats

Bb Major ² Flats

F Major ¹ Flat

C Major ⁰ Flats

The Key of C Major

The C major scale uses the notes C, D, E, F, G, A, B & C.

The Key of C Major

implies -- C, D, E, F, G, A & B.

Signature

CLEFS & KEY SIGNATURE

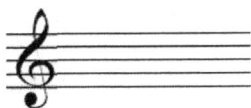

Treble or G clef...

Alto or movable C clef...

Bass or F clef...

Tenor or moveable C clef...

♫ The C major signature has no flats.

Progressions

COMMON PROGRESSIONS

I ⇨ V ⇨ I ...	implies	...	C Maj ⇨ G Maj ⇨ C Maj...
iii ⇨ V ⇨ I ...	implies	...	e min ⇨ G Maj ⇨ C Maj...
I ⇨ IV ⇨ V ⇨ I ...	implies	...	C Maj ⇨ F Maj ⇨ G Maj ⇨ C Maj...
I ⇨ ii ⇨ V ⇨ I ...	implies	...	C Maj ⇨ d min ⇨ G Maj ⇨ C Maj...
I ⇨ vi ⇨ ii ⇨ V ...	implies	...	C Maj ⇨ a min ⇨ d min ⇨ G Maj...
iii ⇨ vi ⇨ ii ⇨ V ...	implies	...	e min ⇨ a min ⇨ d min ⇨ G Maj...

♫ The primary chords are C major Tonic, F major Subdominant & G major Dominant.

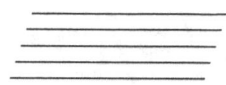

C Triads & Color Tones

The key of A minor is...

Color Tones

DIATONIC CHORD STRUCTURE

6th	A	B	C	D	E	F	G	A
4th	F	G	A	B	C	D	E	F
2nd	D	E	F	G	A	B	C	D
5th ...	G	A	B	C	D	E	F	G
3rd ...	E	F	G	A	B	C	D	E
Root...	C	D	E	F	G	A	B	C
	I	*ii*	*iii*	*IV*	*V*	*vi*	*vii°*	*I*

♫ Any color tone or tones may be voiced with the given triad chord.

Triads

DIATONIC CHORD STRUCTURE

5th ...	G	A	B	C	D	E	F	G
3rd ...	E	F	G	A	B	C	D	E
Root...	C	D	E	F	G	A	B	C
	I	*ii*	*iii*	*IV*	*V*	*vi*	*vii°*	*I*

♫ A triad chord is commonly voiced using just the root & third.

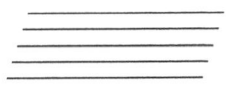

C Sevenths & Extensions

...relative to the key of C major.

Extensions

DIATONIC CHORD STRUCTURE

13th	A	B	C	D	E	F	G	A
11th	F	G	A	B	C	D	E	F
9th	D	E	F	G	A	B	C	D
7th	B	C	D	E	F	G	A	B
5th ...	G	A	B	C	D	E	F	G
3rd ...	E	F	G	A	B	C	D	E
Root...	C	D	E	F	G	A	B	C
	$I^{\triangle 7}$	ii^7	iii^7	$IV^{\triangle 7}$	V^7	vi^7	$vii^{\o 7}$	$I^{\triangle 7}$

♫ Any extension or extensions may be voiced with the given seventh chord.

Sevenths

DIATONIC CHORD STRUCTURE

7th	B	C	D	E	F	G	A	B
5th ...	G	A	B	C	D	E	F	G
3rd ...	E	F	G	A	B	C	D	E
Root...	C	D	E	F	G	A	B	C
	$I^{\triangle 7}$	ii^7	iii^7	$IV^{\triangle 7}$	V^7	vi^7	$vii^{\o 7}$	$I^{\triangle 7}$

♫ A seventh chord is commonly voiced using just the root, third & seventh.

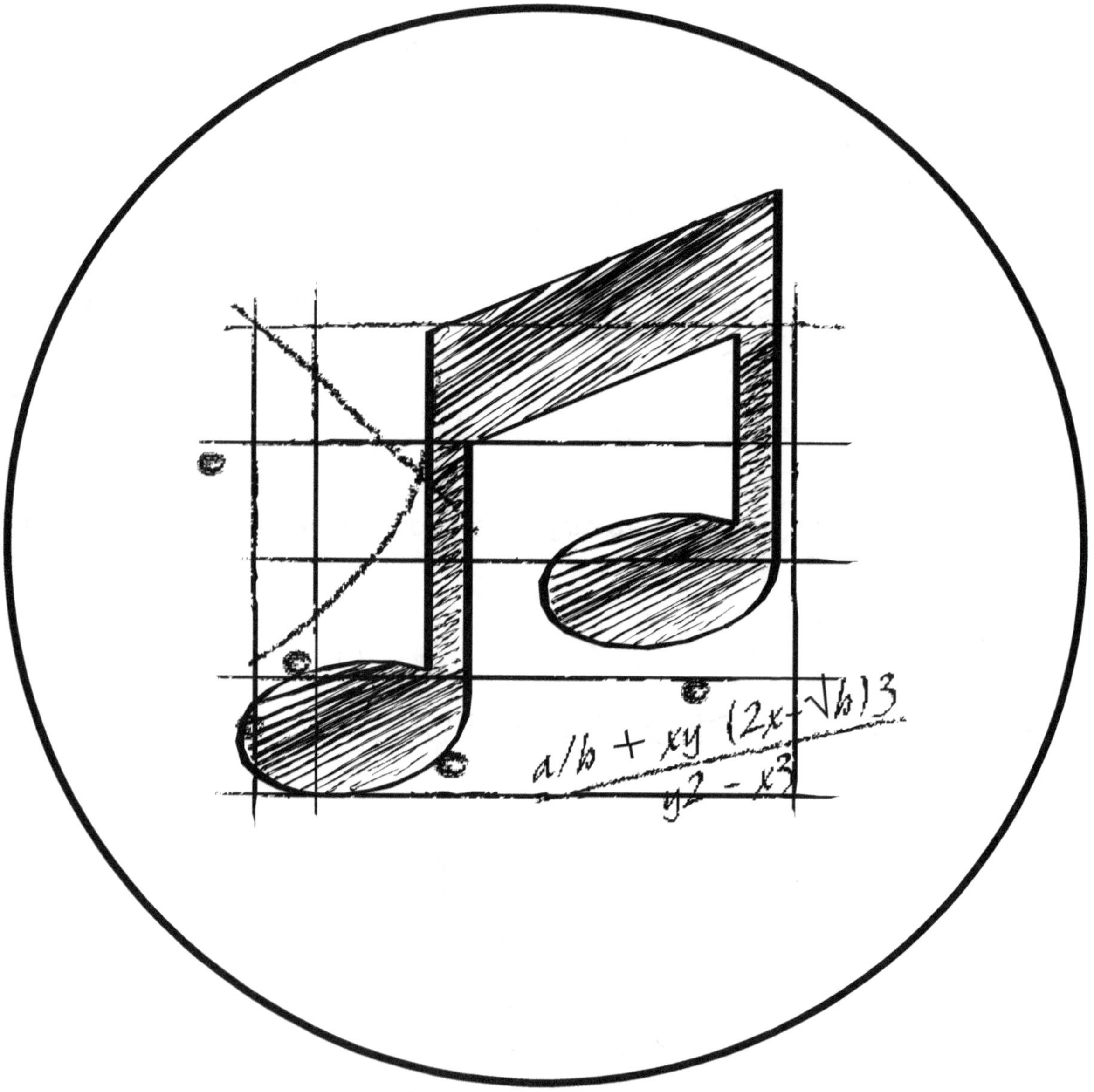
a/b + xy (2x-√b)3
y2 - x3

CHAPTER THREE

The Sharp Minor Keys

A Minor 0 Sharps

E Minor 1 Sharp

B Minor 2 Sharps

F♯ Minor 3 Sharps

C♯ Minor 4 Sharps

G♯ Minor 5 Sharps
A♭ Enharmonic Equivalent

D♯ Minor 6 Sharps
E♭ Enharmonic Equivalent

A♯ Minor 7 Sharps
B♭ Enharmonic Equivalent

The Key of A Minor

The A harmonic minor scale form uses the notes A, B, C, D, E, F, G♯ & A.

The Key of A Minor

implies -- A, B, C, D, E, F & G#.

Signature

CLEFS & KEY SIGNATURE

Treble or G clef...

Alto or movable C clef...

Bass or F clef...

Tenor or movable C clef...

♫ The A minor key signature has no sharps or flats.

Progressions

COMMON PROGRESSIONS

i ⇨ V ⇨ i ...	implies ...	a min ⇨ E Maj ⇨ a min...
III⁺ ⇨ V ⇨ i ...	implies ...	C Aug ⇨ E Maj ⇨ a min...
i ⇨ iv ⇨ V ⇨ i ...	implies ...	a min ⇨ d min ⇨ E Maj ⇨ a min...
i ⇨ ii° ⇨ V ⇨ i ...	implies ...	a min ⇨ b dim ⇨ E Maj ⇨ a min...
i ⇨ VI ⇨ ii° ⇨ V...	implies ...	a min ⇨ F Maj ⇨ b dim ⇨ E Maj...
III⁺ ⇨ VI ⇨ ii° ⇨ V...	implies ...	C Aug ⇨ F Maj ⇨ b dim ⇨ E Maj...

♫ The primary chords are A minor ^Tonic, D minor ^Subdominant & E major ^Dominant.

A Triads & Color Tones

The key of C major is...

Color Tones

DIATONIC CHORD STRUCTURE

6ᵗʰ	F	G♯	A	B	C	D	E	F
4ᵗʰ	D	E	F	G♯	A	B	C	D
2ⁿᵈ	B	C	D	E	F	G♯	A	B
5ᵗʰ ...	E	F	G♯	A	B	C	D	E
3ʳᵈ ...	C	D	E	F	G♯	A	B	C
Root...	A	B	C	D	E	F	G♯	A
	i	*ii°*	*III⁺*	*iv*	*V*	*VI*	*vii°*	*i*

♫ Any color tone or tones may be voiced with the given triad chord.

Triads

DIATONIC CHORD STRUCTURE

5ᵗʰ ...	E	F	G♯	A	B	C	D	E
3ʳᵈ ...	C	D	E	F	G♯	A	B	C
Root...	A	B	C	D	E	F	G♯	A
	i	*ii°*	*III⁺*	*iv*	*V*	*VI*	*vii°*	*i*

♫ A triad chord is commonly voiced using just the root & third.

A Sevenths & Extensions

...relative to the key of A minor.

Extensions
DIATONIC CHORD STRUCTURE

13th	F	G#	A	B	C	D	E	F
11th	D	E	F	G#	A	B	C	D
9th	B	C	D	E	F	G#	A	B
7th	G#	A	B	C	D	E	F	G#
5th ...	E	F	G#	A	B	C	D	E
3rd ...	C	D	E	F	G#	A	B	C
Root...	A	B	C	D	E	F	G#	A
	$i^{\triangle 7}$	$ii^{\emptyset 7}$	$III^{+\triangle 7}$	iv^{7}	V^{7}	$VI^{\triangle 7}$	$vii^{\circ 7}$	$i^{\triangle 7}$

♪ Any extension or extensions may be voiced with the given seventh chord.

Sevenths
DIATONIC CHORD STRUCTURE

7th	G#	A	B	C	D	E	F	G#
5th ...	E	F	G#	A	B	C	D	E
3rd ...	C	D	E	F	G#	A	B	C
Root...	A	B	C	D	E	F	G#	A
	$i^{\triangle 7}$	$ii^{\emptyset 7}$	$III^{+\triangle 7}$	iv^{7}	V^{7}	$VI^{\triangle 7}$	$vii^{\circ 7}$	$i^{\triangle 7}$

♪ A seventh chord is commonly voiced using just the root, third & seventh.

A Minor ^{0 Sharps}

E Minor ^{1 Sharp}

B Minor ^{2 Sharps}

F# Minor ^{3 Sharps}

C# Minor ^{4 Sharps}

G# Minor ^{5 Sharps}
A♭ Enharmonic Equivalent

D# Minor ^{6 Sharps}
E♭ Enharmonic Equivalent

A# Minor ^{7 Sharps}
B♭ Enharmonic Equivalent

The Key of E Minor

The E harmonic minor scale form uses the notes E, F#, G, A, B, C, D# & E.

The Key of E Minor

implies -- E, F♯, G, A, B, C & D♯.

Signature

CLEFS & KEY SIGNATURE

Treble or G clef...

Alto or movable C clef...

Bass or F clef...

Tenor or movable C clef...

♫ The E minor key signature has one sharp -- F♯.

Progressions

COMMON PROGRESSIONS

i ⇨ V ⇨ i ...	implies ...	e min ⇨ B Maj ⇨ e min...
III⁺ ⇨ V ⇨ i ...	implies ...	G Aug ⇨ B Maj ⇨ e min...
i ⇨ iv ⇨ V ⇨ i ...	implies ...	e min ⇨ a min ⇨ B Maj ⇨ e min...
i ⇨ ii° ⇨ V ⇨ i ...	implies ...	e min ⇨ f♯ dim ⇨ B Maj ⇨ e min...
i ⇨ VI ⇨ ii° ⇨ V ...	implies ...	e min ⇨ C Maj ⇨ f♯ dim ⇨ B Maj...
III⁺ ⇨ VI ⇨ ii° ⇨ V ...	implies ...	G Aug ⇨ C Maj ⇨ f♯ dim ⇨ B Maj...

♫ The primary chords are E minor ^{Tonic}, A minor ^{Subdominant} & B major ^{Dominant}.

E Triads & Color Tones

The key of G major is...

Color Tones

DIATONIC CHORD STRUCTURE

6th	C	D♯	E	F♯	G	A	B	C
4th	A	B	C	D♯	E	F♯	G	A
2nd	F♯	G	A	B	C	D♯	E	F♯
5th ...	B	C	D♯	E	F♯	G	A	B
3rd ...	G	A	B	C	D♯	E	F♯	G
Root...	E	F♯	G	A	B	C	D♯	E
	i	*ii°*	*III*⁺	*iv*	*V*	*VI*	*vii°*	*i*

♫ Any color tone or tones may be voiced with the given triad chord.

Triads

DIATONIC CHORD STRUCTURE

5th ...	B	C	D♯	E	F♯	G	A	B
3rd ...	G	A	B	C	D♯	E	F♯	G
Root...	E	F♯	G	A	B	C	D♯	E
	i	*ii°*	*III*⁺	*iv*	*V*	*VI*	*vii°*	*i*

♫ A triad chord is commonly voiced using just the root & third.

E Sevenths & Extensions

...relative to the key of E minor.

Extensions
DIATONIC CHORD STRUCTURE

13th	C	D#	E	F#	G	A	B	C
11th	A	B	C	D#	E	F#	G	A
9th	F#	G	A	B	C	D#	E	F#
7th	D#	E	F#	G	A	B	C	D#
5th ...	B	C	D#	E	F#	G	A	B
3rd ...	G	A	B	C	D#	E	F#	G
Root...	E	F#	G	A	B	C	D#	E
	$i^{\triangle 7}$	$ii^{\varnothing 7}$	$III^{+\triangle 7}$	iv^{7}	V^{7}	$VI^{\triangle 7}$	$vii^{\circ 7}$	$i^{\triangle 7}$

♫ Any extension or extensions may be voiced with the given seventh chord.

Sevenths
DIATONIC CHORD STRUCTURE

7th	D#	E	F#	G	A	B	C	D#
5th ...	B	C	D#	E	F#	G	A	B
3rd ...	G	A	B	C	D#	E	F#	G
Root...	E	F#	G	A	B	C	D#	E
	$i^{\triangle 7}$	$ii^{\varnothing 7}$	$III^{+\triangle 7}$	iv^{7}	V^{7}	$VI^{\triangle 7}$	$vii^{\circ 7}$	$i^{\triangle 7}$

♫ A seventh chord is commonly voiced using just the root, third & seventh.

A Minor ^{0 Sharps}

E Minor ^{1 Sharp}

B Minor ^{2 Sharps}

F# Minor ^{3 Sharps}

C# Minor ^{4 Sharps}

G# Minor ^{5 Sharps}
A♭ Enharmonic Equivalent

D# Minor ^{6 Sharps}
E♭ Enharmonic Equivalent

A# Minor ^{7 Sharps}
B♭ Enharmonic Equivalent

The Key of B Minor

The B harmonic minor scale form uses the notes B, C#, D, E, F#, G, A# & B.

The Key of B Minor

implies -- B, C♯, D, E, F♯, G & A♯.

Signature

CLEFS & KEY SIGNATURE

Treble or G clef...

Alto or movable C clef...

Bass or F clef...

Tenor or movable C clef...

♫ The B minor key signature has two sharps -- F♯ & C♯.

Progressions

COMMON PROGRESSIONS

$i \Rightarrow V \Rightarrow i \ldots$	implies ...	b min ⇨ F♯ Maj ⇨ b min...
$III^+ \Rightarrow V \Rightarrow i \ldots$	implies ...	D Aug ⇨ F♯ Maj ⇨ b min...
$i \Rightarrow iv \Rightarrow V \Rightarrow i \ldots$	implies ...	b min ⇨ e min ⇨ F♯ Maj ⇨ b min...
$i \Rightarrow ii° \Rightarrow V \Rightarrow i \ldots$	implies ...	b min ⇨ c♯ dim ⇨ F♯ Maj ⇨ b min...
$i \Rightarrow VI \Rightarrow ii° \Rightarrow V \ldots$	implies ...	b min ⇨ G Maj ⇨ c♯ dim ⇨ F♯ Maj...
$III^+ \Rightarrow VI \Rightarrow ii° \Rightarrow V \ldots$	implies ...	D Aug ⇨ G Maj ⇨ c♯ dim ⇨ F♯ Maj...

♫ The primary chords are B minor ^{Tonic}, E minor ^{Subdominant} & F♯ major ^{Dominant}.

B Triads & Color Tones

The key of D major is...

Color Tones

DIATONIC CHORD STRUCTURE

6th	G	A#	B	C#	D	E	F#	G
4th	E	F#	G	A#	B	C#	D	E
2nd	C#	D	E	F#	G	A#	B	C#
5th ...	F#	G	A#	B	C#	D	E	F#
3rd ...	D	E	F#	G	A#	B	C#	D
Root...	B	C#	D	E	F#	G	A#	B
	i	*ii°*	*III* +	*iv*	*V*	*VI*	*vii°*	*i*

♫ Any color tone or tones may be voiced with the given triad chord.

Triads

DIATONIC CHORD STRUCTURE

5th ...	F#	G	A#	B	C#	D	E	F#
3rd ...	D	E	F#	G	A#	B	C#	D
Root...	B	C#	D	E	F#	G	A#	B
	i	*ii°*	*III* +	*iv*	*V*	*VI*	*vii°*	*i*

♫ A triad chord is commonly voiced using just the root & third.

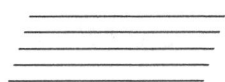

B Sevenths & Extensions

...relative to the key of B minor.

Extensions
DIATONIC CHORD STRUCTURE

13th	G	A#	B	C#	D	E	F#	G
11th	E	F#	G	A#	B	C#	D	E
9th	C#	D	E	F#	G	A#	B	C#
7th	A#	B	C#	D	E	F#	G	A#
5th ...	F#	G	A#	B	C#	D	E	F#
3rd ...	D	E	F#	G	A#	B	C#	D
Root...	B	C#	D	E	F#	G	A#	B
	$i^{\triangle7}$	$ii^{\varnothing7}$	$III^{+\triangle7}$	iv^7	V^7	$VI^{\triangle7}$	$vii^{\circ7}$	$i^{\triangle7}$

♪ Any extension or extensions may be voiced with the given seventh chord.

Sevenths
DIATONIC CHORD STRUCTURE

7th	A#	B	C#	D	E	F#	G	A#
5th ...	F#	G	A#	B	C#	D	E	F#
3rd ...	D	E	F#	G	A#	B	C#	D
Root...	B	C#	D	E	F#	G	A#	B
	$i^{\triangle7}$	$ii^{\varnothing7}$	$III^{+\triangle7}$	iv^7	V^7	$VI^{\triangle7}$	$vii^{\circ7}$	$i^{\triangle7}$

♪ A seventh chord is commonly voiced using just the root, third & seventh.

A Minor ^{0 Sharps}

E Minor ^{1 Sharp}

B Minor ^{2 Sharps}

F# Minor ^{3 Sharps}

C# Minor ^{4 Sharps}

G# Minor ^{5 Sharps}
A♭ Enharmonic Equivalent

D# Minor ^{6 Sharps}
E♭ Enharmonic Equivalent

A# Minor ^{7 Sharps}
B♭ Enharmonic Equivalent

The Key of F# Minor

The F# harmonic minor scale form uses the notes F#, G#, A, B, C#, D, E# & F#.

The Key of F# Minor

implies -- F#, G#, A, B, C#, D & E#.

Signature

CLEFS & KEY SIGNATURE

Treble or G clef...

Alto or movable C clef...

Bass or F clef...

Tenor or movable C clef...

♫ The F# minor key signature has three sharps -- F#, C#, & G#.

Progressions

COMMON PROGRESSIONS

$i \Rightarrow V \Rightarrow i \ldots$	implies	...	f# min ⇨ C# Maj ⇨ f# min...
$III^{+} \Rightarrow V \Rightarrow i \ldots$	implies	...	A Aug ⇨ C# Maj ⇨ f# min...
$i \Rightarrow iv \Rightarrow V \Rightarrow i \ldots$	implies	...	f# min ⇨ b min ⇨ C# Maj ⇨ f# min...
$i \Rightarrow ii° \Rightarrow V \Rightarrow i \ldots$	implies	...	f# min ⇨ g# dim ⇨ C# Maj ⇨ f# min...
$i \Rightarrow VI \Rightarrow ii° \Rightarrow V \ldots$	implies	...	f# min ⇨ D Maj ⇨ g# dim ⇨ C# Maj...
$III^{+} \Rightarrow VI \Rightarrow ii° \Rightarrow V \ldots$	implies	...	A Aug ⇨ D Maj ⇨ g# dim ⇨ C# Maj...

♫ The primary chords are F# minor ᵀᵒⁿⁱᶜ, B minor ˢᵘᵇᵈᵒᵐⁱⁿᵃⁿᵗ & C# major ᴰᵒᵐⁱⁿᵃⁿᵗ.

F# Triads & Color Tones

The key of A major is...

Color Tones

DIATONIC CHORD STRUCTURE

6th	D	E#	F#	G#	A	B	C#	D
4th	B	C#	D	E#	F#	G#	A	B
2nd	G#	A	B	C#	D	E#	F#	G#
5th ...	C#	D	E#	F#	G#	A	B	C#
3rd ...	A	B	C#	D	E#	F#	G#	A
Root...	F#	G#	A	B	C#	D	E#	F#
	i	*ii°*	*III⁺*	*iv*	*V*	*VI*	*vii°*	*i*

♪ Any color tone or tones may be voiced with the given triad chord.

Triads

DIATONIC CHORD STRUCTURE

5th ...	C#	D	E#	F#	G#	A	B	C#
3rd ...	A	B	C#	D	E#	F#	G#	A
Root...	F#	G#	A	B	C#	D	E#	F#
	i	*ii°*	*III⁺*	*iv*	*V*	*VI*	*vii°*	*i*

♪ A triad chord is commonly voiced using just the root & third.

F♯ Sevenths & Extensions

...relative to the key of F♯ minor.

Extensions

DIATONIC CHORD STRUCTURE

13th	D	E♯	F♯	G♯	A	B	C♯	D
11th	B	C♯	D	E♯	F♯	G♯	A	B
9th	G♯	A	B	C♯	D	E♯	F♯	G♯
7th	E♯	F♯	G♯	A	B	C♯	D	E♯
5th …	C♯	D	E♯	F♯	G♯	A	B	C♯
3rd …	A	B	C♯	D	E♯	F♯	G♯	A
Root…	F♯	G♯	A	B	C♯	D	E♯	F♯
	$i^{\triangle 7}$	$ii^{\varnothing 7}$	$III^{+\triangle 7}$	iv^{7}	V^{7}	$VI^{\triangle 7}$	$vii^{\circ 7}$	$i^{\triangle 7}$

♪ Any extension or extensions may be voiced with the given seventh chord.

Sevenths

DIATONIC CHORD STRUCTURE

7th	E♯	F♯	G♯	A	B	C♯	D	E♯
5th …	C♯	D	E♯	F♯	G♯	A	B	C♯
3rd …	A	B	C♯	D	E♯	F♯	G♯	A
Root…	F♯	G♯	A	B	C♯	D	E♯	F♯
	$i^{\triangle 7}$	$ii^{\varnothing 7}$	$III^{+\triangle 7}$	iv^{7}	V^{7}	$VI^{\triangle 7}$	$vii^{\circ 7}$	$i^{\triangle 7}$

♪ A seventh chord is commonly voiced using just the root, third & seventh.

A Minor ^{0 Sharps}

E Minor ^{1 Sharp}

B Minor ^{2 Sharps}

F♯ Minor ^{3 Sharps}

C♯ Minor ^{4 Sharps}

G♯ Minor ^{5 Sharps}
A♭ Enharmonic Equivalent

D♯ Minor ^{6 Sharps}
E♭ Enharmonic Equivalent

A♯ Minor ^{7 Sharps}
B♭ Enharmonic Equivalent

The Key of C♯ Minor

The C♯ harmonic minor scale form uses the notes C♯, D♯, E, F♯, G♯, A, B♯ & C♯.

The Key of C# Minor

implies -- C#, D#, E, F#, G# , A & B#.

Signature

CLEFS & KEY SIGNATURE

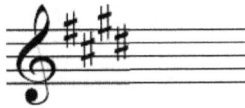

Treble or G clef...

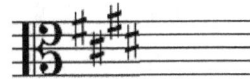

Alto or movable C clef...

Bass or F clef...

Tenor or movable C clef...

♫ The C# minor key signature has four sharps -- F#, C#, G# & D#.

Progressions

COMMON PROGRESSIONS

$i \Rightarrow V \Rightarrow i \ldots$	implies	...	c# min ⇨ G# Maj ⇨ c# min...
$III^{+} \Rightarrow V \Rightarrow i \ldots$	implies	...	E Aug ⇨ G# Maj ⇨ c# min...
$i \Rightarrow iv \Rightarrow V \Rightarrow i \ldots$	implies	...	c# min ⇨ f# min ⇨ G# Maj ⇨ c# min...
$i \Rightarrow ii° \Rightarrow V \Rightarrow i \ldots$	implies	...	c# min ⇨ d# dim ⇨ G# Maj ⇨ c# min...
$i \Rightarrow VI \Rightarrow ii° \Rightarrow V \ldots$	implies	...	c# min ⇨ A Maj ⇨ d# dim ⇨ G# Maj...
$III^{+} \Rightarrow VI \Rightarrow ii° \Rightarrow V \ldots$	implies	...	E Aug ⇨ A Maj ⇨ d# dim ⇨ G# Maj...

♫ The primary chords are C# minor ^Tonic, F# minor ^Subdominant & G# major ^Dominant.

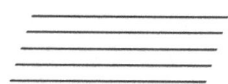

C# Triads & Color Tones

The key of E major is...

Color Tones

DIATONIC CHORD STRUCTURE

6th	A	B#	C#	D#	E	F#	G#	A
4th	F#	G#	A	B#	C#	D#	E	F#
2nd	D#	E	F#	G#	A	B#	C#	D#
5th ...	G#	A	B#	C#	D#	E	F#	G#
3rd ...	E	F#	G#	A	B#	C#	D#	E
Root...	C#	D#	E	F#	G#	A	B#	C#
	i	*ii°*	*III⁺*	*iv*	*V*	*VI*	*vii°*	*i*

♫ Any color tone or tones may be voiced with the given triad chord.

Triads

DIATONIC CHORD STRUCTURE

5th ...	G#	A	B#	C#	D#	E	F#	G#
3rd ...	E	F#	G#	A	B#	C#	D#	E
Root...	C#	D#	E	F#	G#	A	B#	C#
	i	*ii°*	*III⁺*	*iv*	*V*	*VI*	*vii°*	*i*

♫ A triad chord is commonly voiced using just the root & third.

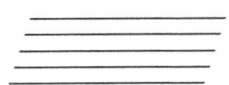

C# Sevenths & Extensions

...relative to the key of C# minor.

Extensions

DIATONIC CHORD STRUCTURE

13th	A	B#	C#	D#	E	F#	G#	A
11th	F#	G#	A	B#	C#	D#	E	F#
9th	D#	E	F#	G#	A	B#	C#	D#
7th	B#	C#	D#	E	F#	G#	A	B#
5th ...	G#	A	B#	C#	D#	E	F#	G#
3rd ...	E	F#	G#	A	B#	C#	D#	E
Root...	C#	D#	E	F#	G#	A	B#	C#
	$i^{\triangle 7}$	$ii^{\o 7}$	$III^{+\triangle 7}$	iv^7	V^7	$VI^{\triangle 7}$	$vii^{\circ 7}$	$i^{\triangle 7}$

♪ Any extension or extensions may be voiced with the given seventh chord.

Sevenths

DIATONIC CHORD STRUCTURE

7th	B#	C#	D#	E	F#	G#	A	B#
5th ...	G#	A	B#	C#	D#	E	F#	G#
3rd ...	E	F#	G#	A	B#	C#	D#	E
Root...	C#	D#	E	F#	G#	A	B#	C#
	$i^{\triangle 7}$	$ii^{\o 7}$	$III^{+\triangle 7}$	iv^7	V^7	$VI^{\triangle 7}$	$vii^{\circ 7}$	$i^{\triangle 7}$

♪ A seventh chord is commonly voiced using just the root, third & seventh.

A Minor ^{0 Sharps}

E Minor ^{1 Sharp}

B Minor ^{2 Sharps}

F# Minor ^{3 Sharps}

C# Minor ^{4 Sharps}

G# Minor ^{5 Sharps}
Ab Enharmonic Equivalent

D# Minor ^{6 Sharps}
Eb Enharmonic Equivalent

A# Minor ^{7 Sharps}
Bb Enharmonic Equivalent

The Key of G# Minor

The G#, harmonic minor scale form uses the notes G#,, A#,, B, C#,, D#,, E, Fx & G#,.

The Key of G♯ Minor

implies -- G♯, A♯, B, C♯, D♯, E & Fx.

Signature

CLEFS & KEY SIGNATURE

Treble or G clef...

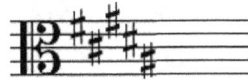

Alto or movable C clef...

Bass or F clef...

Tenor or movable C clef...

♫ The G♯ minor key signature has five sharps -- F♯, C♯, G♯, D♯ & A♯.

Progressions

COMMON PROGRESSIONS

i ⇨ V ⇨ i ...	implies ...	g♯ min ⇨ D♯ Maj ⇨ g♯ min...
III⁺ ⇨ V ⇨ i ...	implies ...	B Aug ⇨ D♯ Maj ⇨ g♯ min...
i ⇨ iv ⇨ V ⇨ i ...	implies ...	g♯ min ⇨ c♯ min ⇨ D♯ Maj ⇨ g♯ min...
i ⇨ ii° ⇨ V ⇨ i ...	implies ...	g♯ min ⇨ a♯ dim ⇨ D♯ Maj ⇨ g♯ min...
i ⇨ VI ⇨ ii° ⇨ V...	implies ...	g♯ min ⇨ E Maj ⇨ a♯ dim ⇨ D♯ Maj...
III⁺ ⇨ VI ⇨ ii° ⇨ V...	implies ...	B Aug ⇨ E Maj ⇨ a♯ dim ⇨ D♯ Maj...

♫ The primary chords are G♯ minor ᵀᵒⁿⁱᶜ, C♯ minor ˢᵘᵇᵈᵒᵐⁱⁿᵃⁿᵗ & D♯ major ᴰᵒᵐⁱⁿᵃⁿᵗ.

G# Triads & Color Tones

The key of B major is...

Color Tones
DIATONIC CHORD STRUCTURE

6th	E	Fx	G#	A#	B	C#	D#	E
4th	C#	D#	E	Fx	G#	A#	B	C#
2nd	A#	B	C#	D#	E	Fx	G#	A#
5th ...	D#	E	Fx	G#	A#	B	C#	D#
3rd ...	B	C#	D#	E	Fx	G#	A#	B
Root...	G#	A#	B	C#	D#	E	Fx	G#
	i	ii°	III +	iv	V	VI	vii°	i

♪ Any color tone or tones may be voiced with the given triad chord.

Triads
DIATONIC CHORD STRUCTURE

5th ...	D#	E	Fx	G#	A#	B	C#	D#
3rd ...	B	C#	D#	E	Fx	G#	A#	B
Root...	G#	A#	B	C#	D#	E	Fx	G#
	i	ii°	III +	iv	V	VI	vii°	i

♪ A triad chord is commonly voiced using just the root & third.

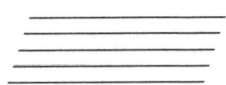

G# Sevenths & Extensions

...relative to the key of G# minor.

Extensions
DIATONIC CHORD STRUCTURE

13th	E	Fx	G#	A#	B	C#	D#	E
11th	C#	D#	E	Fx	G#	A#	B	C#
9th	A#	B	C#	D#	E	Fx	G#	A#
7th	Fx	G#	A#	B	C#	D#	E	Fx
5th ...	D#	E	Fx	G#	A#	B	C#	D#
3rd ...	B	C#	D#	E	Fx	G#	A#	B
Root...	G#	A#	B	C#	D#	E	Fx	G#
	$i^{\triangle 7}$	$ii^{\varnothing 7}$	$III^{+\triangle 7}$	iv^7	V^7	$VI^{\triangle 7}$	$vii^{\circ 7}$	$i^{\triangle 7}$

♫ Any extension or extensions may be voiced with the given seventh chord.

Sevenths
DIATONIC CHORD STRUCTURE

7th	Fx	G#	A#	B	C#	D#	E	Fx
5th ...	D#	E	Fx	G#	A#	B	C#	D#
3rd ...	B	C#	D#	E	Fx	G#	A#	B
Root...	G#	A#	B	C#	D#	E	Fx	G#
	$i^{\triangle 7}$	$ii^{\varnothing 7}$	$III^{+\triangle 7}$	iv^7	V^7	$VI^{\triangle 7}$	$vii^{\circ 7}$	$i^{\triangle 7}$

♫ A seventh chord is commonly voiced using just the root, third & seventh.

A Minor ^{0 Sharps}

E Minor ^{1 Sharp}

B Minor ^{2 Sharps}

F♯ Minor ^{3 Sharps}

C♯ Minor ^{4 Sharps}

G♯ Minor ^{5 Sharps}
A♭ Enharmonic Equivalent

D♯ Minor ^{6 Sharps}
E♭ Enharmonic Equivalent

A♯ Minor ^{7 Sharps}
B♭ Enharmonic Equivalent

The Key of D♯ Minor

The D♯ harmonic minor scale form uses the notes D♯, E♯, F♯, G♯, A♯, B, Cx & D♯.

The Key of D♯ Minor

implies -- D♯, E♯, F♯, G♯, A♯, B & Cx.

Signature

CLEFS & KEY SIGNATURE

Treble or G clef...

Alto or movable C clef...

Bass or F clef...

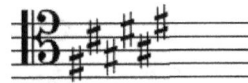

Tenor or movable C clef...

♪ The D♯ minor key signature has six sharps -- F♯, C♯, G♯, D♯, A♯ & E♯.

Progressions

COMMON PROGRESSIONS

i ⇨ V ⇨ i ...	implies ...	d♯ min ⇨ A♯ Maj ⇨ d♯ min...
III⁺ ⇨ V ⇨ i ...	implies ...	F♯ Aug ⇨ A♯ Maj ⇨ d♯ min...
i ⇨ iv ⇨ V ⇨ i ...	implies ...	d♯ min ⇨ g♯ min ⇨ A♯ Maj ⇨ d♯ min...
i ⇨ ii° ⇨ V ⇨ i ...	implies ...	d♯ min ⇨ e♯ dim ⇨ A♯ Maj ⇨ d♯ min...
i ⇨ VI ⇨ ii° ⇨ V ...	implies ...	d♯ min ⇨ B Maj ⇨ e♯ dim ⇨ A♯ Maj...
III⁺ ⇨ VI ⇨ ii° ⇨ V ...implies ...		F♯ Aug ⇨ B Maj ⇨ e♯ dim ⇨ A♯ Maj...

♪ The primary chords are D♯ minor ^Tonic^, G♯ minor ^Subdominant^ & A♯ major ^Dominant^.

UNABRIDGED DIATONICS™   A COMPLETE DIATONIC REFERENCE – THE CIRCLE OF FIFTHS   COPYRIGHT © 2011 OMNI MUSIC PRESS®

D♯ Triads & Color Tones

The key of F♯ major is...

Color Tones

DIATONIC CHORD STRUCTURE

6th	B	C×	D♯	E♯	F♯	G♯	A♯	B
4th	G♯	A♯	B	C×	D♯	E♯	F♯	D♯
2nd	E♯	F♯	G♯	A♯	B	C×	D♯	E♯
5th ...	A♯	B	C×	D♯	E♯	F♯	G♯	A♯
3rd ...	F♯	G♯	A♯	B	C×	D♯	E♯	F♯
Root...	D♯	E♯	F♯	G♯	A♯	B	C×	D♯
	i	*ii°*	*III⁺*	*iv*	*V*	*VI*	*vii°*	*i*

♪ Any color tone or tones may be voiced with the given triad chord.

Triads

DIATONIC CHORD STRUCTURE

5th ...	A♯	B	C×	D♯	E♯	F♯	G♯	A♯
3rd ...	F♯	G♯	A♯	B	C×	D♯	E♯	F♯
Root...	D♯	E♯	F♯	G♯	A♯	B	C×	D♯
	i	*ii°*	*III⁺*	*iv*	*V*	*VI*	*vii°*	*i*

♪ A triad chord is commonly voiced using just the root & third.

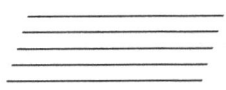

D♯ Sevenths & Extensions

...relative to the key of D♯ minor.

E x t e n s i o n s

DIATONIC CHORD STRUCTURE

13th	B	C×	D♯	E♯	F♯	G♯	A♯	B
11th	G♯	A♯	B	C×	D♯	E♯	F♯	D♯
9th	E♯	F♯	G♯	A♯	B	C×	D♯	E♯
7th	C×	D♯	E♯	F♯	G♯	A♯	B	C×
5th ...	A♯	B	C×	D♯	E♯	F♯	G♯	A♯
3rd ...	F♯	G♯	A♯	B	C×	D♯	E♯	F♯
Root...	D♯	E♯	F♯	G♯	A♯	B	C×	D♯
	$i^{\triangle 7}$	$ii^{\varnothing 7}$	$III^{+\triangle 7}$	iv^{7}	V^{7}	$VI^{\triangle 7}$	$vii^{\circ 7}$	$i^{\triangle 7}$

♫ Any extension or extensions may be voiced with the given seventh chord.

S e v e n t h s

DIATONIC CHORD STRUCTURE

7th	C×	D♯	E♯	F♯	G♯	A♯	B	C×
5th ...	A♯	B	C×	D♯	E♯	F♯	G♯	A♯
3rd ...	F♯	G♯	A♯	B	C×	D♯	E♯	F♯
Root...	D♯	E♯	F♯	G♯	A♯	B	C×	D♯
	$i^{\triangle 7}$	$ii^{\varnothing 7}$	$III^{+\triangle 7}$	iv^{7}	V^{7}	$VI^{\triangle 7}$	$vii^{\circ 7}$	$i^{\triangle 7}$

♫ A seventh chord is commonly voiced using just the root, third & seventh.

A Minor ^{0 Sharps}

E Minor ^{1 Sharp}

B Minor ^{2 Sharps}

F♯ Minor ^{3 Sharps}

C♯ Minor ^{4 Sharps}

G♯ Minor ^{5 Sharps}
A♭ Enharmonic Equivalent

D♯ Minor ^{6 Sharps}
E♭ Enharmonic Equivalent

A♯ Minor ^{7 Sharps}
B♭ Enharmonic Equivalent

The Key of A♯ Minor

The A♯ harmonic minor scale form uses the notes A♯, B♯, C♯, D♯, E♯, F♯, Gⓧ & A♯.

The Key of A♯ Minor

implies -- A♯, B♯, C♯, D♯, E♯, F♯ & Gx.

Signature

CLEFS & KEY SIGNATURE

Treble or G clef...

Alto or movable C clef...

Bass or F clef...

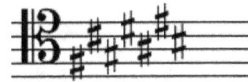

Tenor or movable C clef...

♫ The A♯ minor key signature has seven sharps -- F♯, C♯, G♯, D♯, A♯, E♯ & B♯.

Progressions

COMMON PROGRESSIONS

i ⇨ *V* ⇨ *i* ...	implies ...	a♯ min ⇨ E♯ Maj ⇨ a♯ min...
III ⁺ ⇨ *V* ⇨ *i* ...	implies ...	C♯ Aug ⇨ E♯ Maj ⇨ a♯ min...
i ⇨ *iv* ⇨ *V* ⇨ *i* ...	implies ...	a♯ min ⇨ d♯ min ⇨ E♯ Maj ⇨ a♯ min...
i ⇨ *ii°* ⇨ *V* ⇨ *i* ...	implies ...	a♯ min ⇨ b♯ dim ⇨ E♯ Maj ⇨ a♯ min...
i ⇨ *VI* ⇨ *ii°* ⇨ *V*...	implies ...	a♯ min ⇨ F♯ Maj ⇨ b♯ dim ⇨ E♯ Maj...
III ⁺ ⇨ *VI* ⇨ *ii°* ⇨ *V*...implies	...	C♯ Aug ⇨ F♯ Maj ⇨ b♯ dim ⇨ E♯ Maj...

♫ The primary chords are A♯ minor ^Tonic, D♯ minor ^Subdominant & E♯ major ^Dominant.

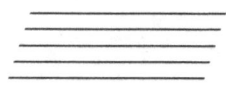

A♯ Triads & Color Tones

The key of C♯ major is...

Color Tones

DIATONIC CHORD STRUCTURE

6th	F♯	G𝄪	A♯	B♯	C♯	D♯	E♯	F♯
4th	D♯	E♯	F♯	G𝄪	A♯	B♯	C♯	D♯
2nd	B♯	C♯	D♯	E♯	F♯	G𝄪	A♯	B♯
5th ...	E♯	F♯	G𝄪	A♯	B♯	C♯	D♯	E♯
3rd ...	C♯	D♯	E♯	F♯	G𝄪	A♯	B♯	C♯
Root...	A♯	B♯	C♯	D♯	E♯	F♯	G𝄪	A♯
	i	$ii°$	III^+	iv	V	VI	$vii°$	i

♪ Any color tone or tones may be voiced with the given triad chord.

Triads

DIATONIC CHORD STRUCTURE

5th ...	E♯	F♯	G𝄪	A♯	B♯	C♯	D♯	E♯
3rd ...	C♯	D♯	E♯	F♯	G𝄪	A♯	B♯	C♯
Root...	A♯	B♯	C♯	D♯	E♯	F♯	G𝄪	A♯
	i	$ii°$	III^+	iv	V	VI	$vii°$	i

♪ A triad chord is commonly voiced using just the root & third.

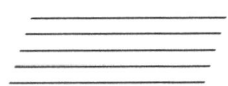

A♯ Sevenths & Extensions

...relative to the key of A♯ minor.

Extensions

DIATONIC CHORD STRUCTURE

13th	F♯	G𝄪	A♯	B♯	C♯	D♯	E♯	F♯
11th	D♯	E♯	F♯	G𝄪	A♯	B♯	C♯	D♯
9th	B♯	C♯	D♯	E♯	F♯	G𝄪	A♯	B♯
7th	G𝄪	A♯	B♯	C♯	D♯	E♯	F♯	G𝄪
5th ...	E♯	F♯	G𝄪	A♯	B♯	C♯	D♯	E♯
3rd ...	C♯	D♯	E♯	F♯	G𝄪	A♯	B♯	C♯
Root...	A♯	B♯	C♯	D♯	E♯	F♯	G𝄪	A♯
	$i^{\triangle 7}$	$ii^{\o 7}$	$III^{+\triangle 7}$	iv^{7}	V^{7}	$VI^{\triangle 7}$	$vii^{\circ 7}$	$i^{\triangle 7}$

♫ Any extension or extensions may be voiced with the given seventh chord.

Sevenths

DIATONIC CHORD STRUCTURE

7th	G𝄪	A♯	B♯	C♯	D♯	E♯	F♯	G𝄪
5th ...	E♯	F♯	G𝄪	A♯	B♯	C♯	D♯	E♯
3rd ...	C♯	D♯	E♯	F♯	G𝄪	A♯	B♯	C♯
Root...	A♯	B♯	C♯	D♯	E♯	F♯	G𝄪	A♯
	$i^{\triangle 7}$	$ii^{\o 7}$	$III^{+\triangle 7}$	iv^{7}	V^{7}	$VI^{\triangle 7}$	$vii^{\circ 7}$	$i^{\triangle 7}$

♫ A seventh chord is commonly voiced using just the root, third & seventh.

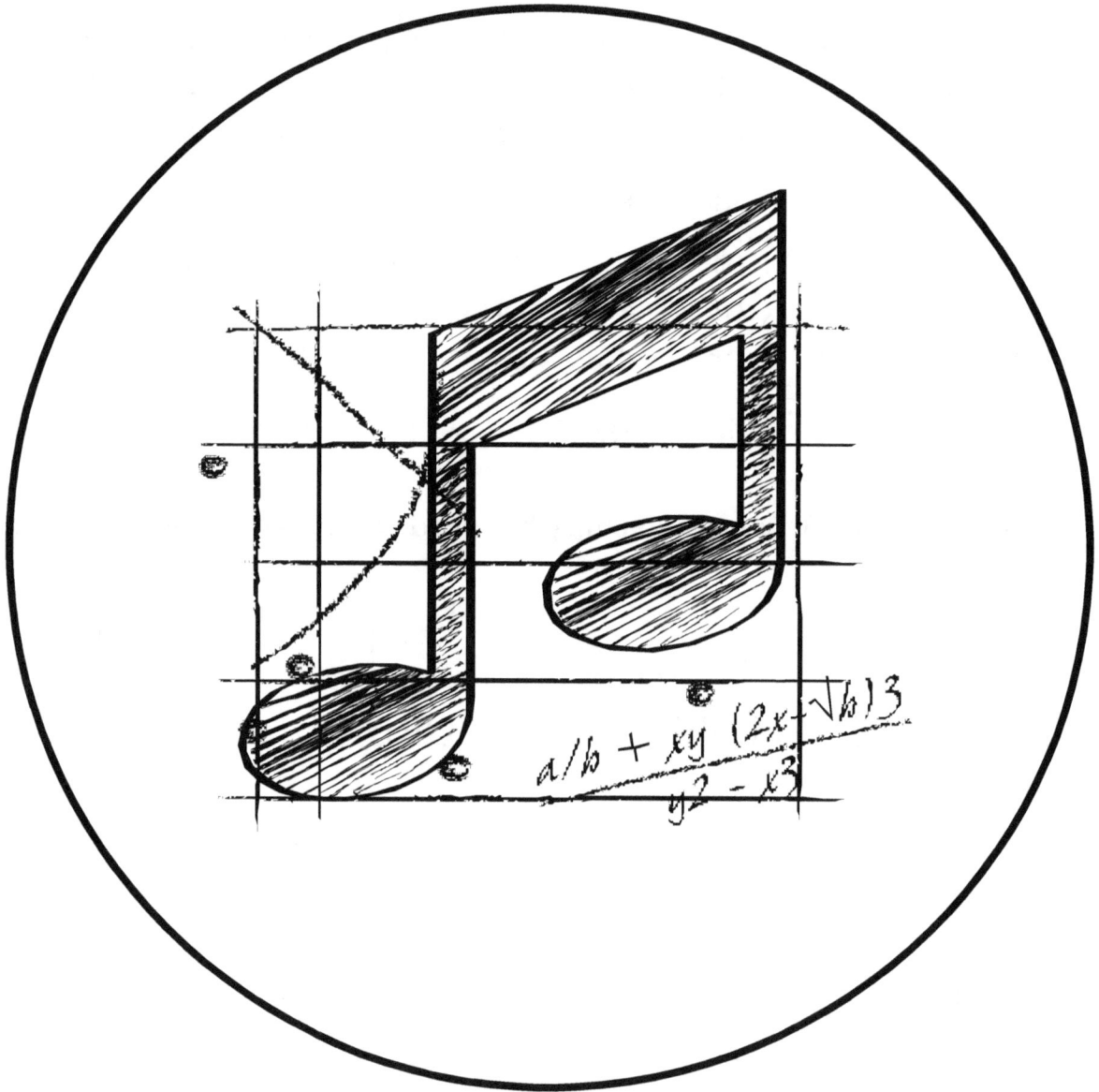

CHAPTER FOUR

The Flat Minor Keys

Ab Minor 7 Flats

Eb Minor 6 Flats

Bb Minor 5 Flats

F Minor 4 Flats

C Minor 3 Flats

G Minor 2 Flats

D Minor 1 Flat

A Minor 0 Flats

The Key of Ab Minor

The Ab harmonic minor scale form uses the notes Ab, Bb, Cb, Db, Eb, Fb, G♮ & Ab.

The Key of A♭ Minor

implies -- A♭, B♭, C♭, D♭, E♭, F♭ & G♮.

Signature

CLEFS & KEY SIGNATURE

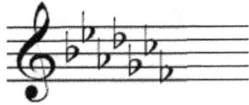

Treble or G clef...

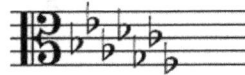

Alto or movable C clef...

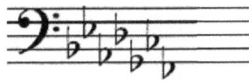

Bass or F clef...

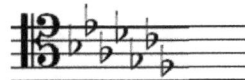

Tenor or movable C clef...

♫ The A♭ minor signature has seven flats -- B♭, E♭, A♭, D♭, G♭, C♭ & F♭.

Progressions

COMMON PROGRESSIONS

$i \Rightarrow V \Rightarrow i$ ...	implies ...	a♭ min ⇨ E♭ Maj ⇨ a♭ min...
$III^+ \Rightarrow V \Rightarrow i$ ...	implies ...	C♭ Aug ⇨ E♭ Maj ⇨ a♭ min...
$i \Rightarrow iv \Rightarrow V \Rightarrow i$ ...	implies ...	a♭ min ⇨ d♭ min ⇨ E♭ Maj ⇨ a♭ min...
$i \Rightarrow ii° \Rightarrow V \Rightarrow i$ ...	implies ...	a♭ min ⇨ b♭ dim ⇨ E♭ Maj ⇨ a♭ min...
$i \Rightarrow VI \Rightarrow ii° \Rightarrow V$ ...	implies ...	a♭ min ⇨ F♭ Maj ⇨ b♭ dim ⇨ E♭ Maj...
$III^+ \Rightarrow VI \Rightarrow ii° \Rightarrow V$ ...	implies ...	C♭ Aug ⇨ F♭ Maj ⇨ b♭ dim ⇨ E♭ Maj...

♫ The primary chords are A♭ minor [Tonic], D♭ minor [Subdominant] & E♭ major [Dominant].

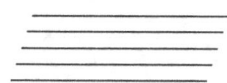

A♭ Triads & Color Tones

The key of C♭ major is...

Color Tones

DIATONIC CHORD STRUCTURE

6th	F♭	G♮	A♭	B♭	C♭	D♭	E♭	F♭
4th	D♭	E♭	F♭	G♮	A♭	B♭	C♭	D♭
2nd	B♭	C♭	D♭	E♭	F♭	G♮	A♭	B♭
5th ...	E♭	F♭	G♮	A♭	B♭	C♭	D♭	E♭
3rd ...	C♭	D♭	E♭	F♭	G♮	A♭	B♭	C♭
Root...	A♭	B♭	C♭	D♭	E♭	F♭	G♮	A♭
	i	*ii°*	*III⁺*	*iv*	*V*	*VI*	*vii°*	*i*

♫ Any color tone or tones may be voiced with the given triad chord.

Triads

DIATONIC CHORD STRUCTURE

5th ...	E♭	F♭	G♮	A♭	B♭	C♭	D♭	E♭
3rd ...	C♭	D♭	E♭	F♭	G♮	A♭	B♭	C♭
Root...	A♭	B♭	C♭	D♭	E♭	F♭	G♮	A♭
	i	*ii°*	*III⁺*	*iv*	*V*	*VI*	*vii°*	*i*

♫ A triad chord is commonly voiced using just the root & third.

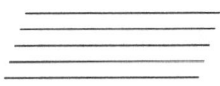

A♭ Seventhsths & Extensions

...relative to the key of A♭ minor.

Extensions
DIATONIC CHORD STRUCTURE

13th	F♭	G♮	A♭	B♭	C♭	D♭	E♭	F♭
11th	D♭	E♭	F♭	G♮	A♭	B♭	C♭	D♭
9th	B♭	C♭	D♭	E♭	F♭	G♮	A♭	B♭
7th	G♮	A♭	B♭	C♭	D♭	E♭	F♭	G♮
5th ...	E♭	F♭	G♮	A♭	B♭	C♭	D♭	E♭
3rd ...	C♭	D♭	E♭	F♭	G♮	A♭	B♭	C♭
Root...	A♭	B♭	C♭	D♭	E♭	F♭	G♮	A♭
	$i^{\triangle 7}$	$ii^{\varnothing 7}$	$III^{+\triangle 7}$	iv^7	V^7	$VI^{\triangle 7}$	$vii^{\circ 7}$	$i^{\triangle 7}$

♫ Any extension or extensions may be voiced with the given seventh chord.

Sevenths
DIATONIC CHORD STRUCTURE

7th	G♮	A♭	B♭	C♭	D♭	E♭	F♭	G♮
5th ...	E♭	F♭	G♮	A♭	B♭	C♭	D♭	E♭
3rd ...	C♭	D♭	E♭	F♭	G♮	A♭	B♭	C♭
Root...	A♭	B♭	C♭	D♭	E♭	F♭	G♮	A♭
	$i^{\triangle 7}$	$ii^{\varnothing 7}$	$III^{+\triangle 7}$	iv^7	V^7	$VI^{\triangle 7}$	$vii^{\circ 7}$	$i^{\triangle 7}$

♫ A seventh chord is commonly voiced using just the root, third & seventh.

Ab Minor ⁷ Flats

Eb Minor ⁶ Flats

Bb Minor ⁵ Flats

F Minor ⁴ Flats

C Minor ³ Flats

G Minor ² Flats

D Minor ¹ Flat

A Minor ⁰ Flats

The Key of Eb Minor

The Eb harmonic minor scale form uses the notes Eb, F, Gb, Ab, Bb, Cb, Db & Eb.

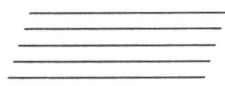

The Key of E♭ Minor

implies -- E♭, F, G♭, A♭, B♭, C♭ & D♮.

Signature

CLEFS & KEY SIGNATURE

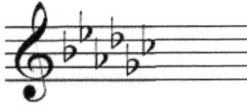

Treble or G clef...

Alto or movable C clef...

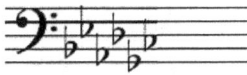

Bass or F clef...

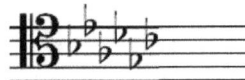

Tenor or movable C clef...

♪ The E♭ minor signature has six flats -- B♭, E♭, A♭, D♭, G♭ & C♭.

Progressions

COMMON PROGRESSIONS

i ⇨ V ⇨ i ...	implies ...	e♭ min ⇨ B♭ Maj ⇨ e♭ min...
III⁺ ⇨ V ⇨ i ...	implies ...	G♭ Aug ⇨ B♭ Maj ⇨ e♭ min...
i ⇨ iv ⇨ V ⇨ i ...	implies ...	e♭ min ⇨ a♭ min ⇨ B♭ Maj ⇨ e♭ min...
i ⇨ ii° ⇨ V ⇨ i ...	implies ...	e♭ min ⇨ f dim ⇨ B♭ Maj ⇨ e♭ min...
i ⇨ VI ⇨ ii° ⇨ V...	implies ...	e♭ min ⇨ C♭ Maj ⇨ f dim ⇨ B♭ Maj...
III⁺ ⇨ VI ⇨ ii° ⇨ V...	implies ...	G♭ Aug ⇨ C♭ Maj ⇨ f dim ⇨ B♭ Maj...

♪ The primary chords are E♭ minor ᵀᵒⁿⁱᶜ, A♭ minor ˢᵘᵇᵈᵒᵐⁱⁿᵃⁿᵗ & B♭ major ᴰᵒᵐⁱⁿᵃⁿᵗ.

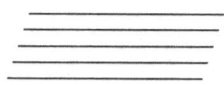

Eb Triads & Color Tones

The key of Gb major is...

Color Tones

DIATONIC CHORD STRUCTURE

6th	Cb	D♮	Eb	F	Gb	Ab	Bb	Cb
4th	Ab	Bb	Cb	D♮	Eb	F	Gb	Ab
2nd	F	Gb	Ab	Bb	Cb	D♮	Eb	F

5th …	Bb	Cb	D♮	Eb	F	Gb	Ab	Bb
3rd …	Gb	Ab	Bb	Cb	D♮	Eb	F	Gb
Root…	Eb	F	Gb	Ab	Bb	Cb	D♮	Eb
	i	*ii°*	*III+*	*iv*	*V*	*VI*	*vii°*	*i*

♪ Any color tone or tones may be voiced with the given triad chord.

Triads

DIATONIC CHORD STRUCTURE

5th …	Bb	Cb	D♮	Eb	F	Gb	Ab	Bb
3rd …	Gb	Ab	Bb	Cb	D♮	Eb	F	Gb
Root…	Eb	F	Gb	Ab	Bb	Cb	D♮	Eb
	i	*ii°*	*III+*	*iv*	*V*	*VI*	*vii°*	*i*

♪ A triad chord is commonly voiced using just the root & third.

E♭ Sevenths & Extensions

...relative to the key of E♭ minor.

Extensions

DIATONIC CHORD STRUCTURE

13th	C♭	D♮	E♭	F	G♭	A♭	B♭	C♭
11th	A♭	B♭	C♭	D♮	E♭	F	G♭	A♭
9th	F	G♭	A♭	B♭	C♭	D♮	E♭	F
7th	D♮	E♭	F	G♭	A♭	B♭	C♭	D♮
5th ...	B♭	C♭	D♮	E♭	F	G♭	A♭	B♭
3rd ...	G♭	A♭	B♭	C♭	D♮	E♭	F	G♭
Root...	E♭	F	G♭	A♭	B♭	C♭	D♮	E♭
	$i^{\triangle 7}$	$ii^{\emptyset 7}$	$III^{+\triangle 7}$	iv^{7}	V^{7}	$VI^{\triangle 7}$	$vii^{\circ 7}$	$i^{\triangle 7}$

♫ Any extension or extensions may be voiced with the given seventh chord.

Sevenths

DIATONIC CHORD STRUCTURE

7th	A♮	B♭	C	D♭	E♭	F	G♭	A♮
5th ...	B♭	C♭	D♮	E♭	F	G♭	A♭	B♭
3rd ...	G♭	A♭	B♭	C♭	D♮	E♭	F	G♭
Root...	E♭	F	G♭	A♭	B♭	C♭	D♮	E♭
	$i^{\triangle 7}$	$ii^{\emptyset 7}$	$III^{+\triangle 7}$	iv^{7}	V^{7}	$VI^{\triangle 7}$	$vii^{\circ 7}$	$i^{\triangle 7}$

♫ A seventh chord is commonly voiced using just the root, third & seventh.

A♭ Minor ^{7 Flats}

E♭ Minor ^{6 Flats}

B♭ Minor ^{5 Flats}

F Minor ^{4 Flats}

C Minor ^{3 Flats}

G Minor ^{2 Flats}

D Minor ^{1 Flat}

A Minor ^{0 Flats}

The Key of B♭ Minor

The B♭ harmonic minor scale form uses the notes B♭, C, D♭, E♭, F, G♭, A♮ & B♭.

The Key of B♭ Minor

implies -- B♭, C, D♭, E♭, F, G♭ & A♮.

Signature

CLEFS & KEY SIGNATURE

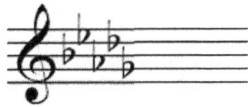

Treble or G clef...

Alto or movable C clef...

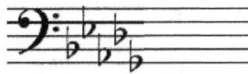

Bass or F clef...

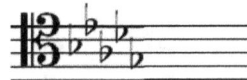

Tenor or movable C clef...

♫ The B♭ minor signature has five flats -- B♭, E♭, A♭, D♭ & G♭.

Progressions

COMMON PROGRESSIONS

i ⇨ V ⇨ i ...	implies	...	b♭ min ⇨ F Maj ⇨ b♭ min...
III⁺ ⇨ V ⇨ i ...	implies	...	D♭ Aug ⇨ F Maj ⇨ b♭ min...
i ⇨ iv ⇨ V ⇨ i ...	implies	...	b♭ min ⇨ e♭ min ⇨ F Maj ⇨ b♭ min...
i ⇨ ii° ⇨ V ⇨ i ...	implies	...	b♭ min ⇨ c dim ⇨ F Maj ⇨ b♭ min...
i ⇨ VI ⇨ ii° ⇨ V...	implies	...	b♭ min ⇨ G♭ Maj ⇨ c dim ⇨ F Maj...
III⁺ ⇨ VI ⇨ ii° ⇨ V...implies		...	D♭ Aug ⇨ G♭ Maj ⇨ c dim ⇨ F Maj...

♫ The primary chords are B♭ minor ᵀᵒⁿⁱᶜ, E♭ minor ˢᵘᵇᵈᵒᵐⁱⁿᵃⁿᵗ & F major ᴰᵒᵐⁱⁿᵃⁿᵗ.

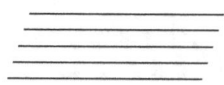

B♭ Triads & Color Tones

The key of D♭ major is...

Color Tones

DIATONIC CHORD STRUCTURE

6th	G♭	A♮	B♭	C	D♭	E♭	F	G♭
4th	E♭	F	G♭	A♮	B♭	C	D♭	E♭
2nd	C	D♭	E♭	F	G♭	A♮	B♭	C
5th ...	F	G♭	A♮	B♭	C	D♭	E♭	F
3rd ...	D♭	E♭	F	G♭	A♮	B♭	C	D♭
Root...	B♭	C	D♭	E♭	F	G♭	A♮	B♭
	i	*ii°*	*III⁺*	*iv*	*V*	*VI*	*vii°*	*i*

♪ Any color tone or tones may be voiced with the given triad chord.

Triads

DIATONIC CHORD STRUCTURE

5th ...	F	G♭	A♮	B♭	C	D♭	E♭	F
3rd ...	D♭	E♭	F	G♭	A♮	B♭	C	D♭
Root...	B♭	C	D♭	E♭	F	G♭	A♮	B♭
	i	*ii°*	*III⁺*	*iv*	*V*	*VI*	*vii°*	*i*

♪ A triad chord is commonly voiced using just the root & third.

Bb Sevenths & Extensions

...relative to the key of Bb minor.

Extensions
DIATONIC CHORD STRUCTURE

	$i^{\triangle 7}$	$ii^{\emptyset 7}$	$III^{+\triangle 7}$	iv^{7}	V^{7}	$VI^{\triangle 7}$	$vii^{\circ 7}$	$i^{\triangle 7}$
13th	Gb	A♮	Bb	C	Db	Eb	F	Gb
11th	Eb	F	Gb	A♮	Bb	C	Db	Eb
9th	C	Db	Eb	F	Gb	A♮	Bb	C
7th	A♮	Bb	C	Db	Eb	F	Gb	A♮
5th ...	F	Gb	A♮	Bb	C	Db	Eb	F
3rd ...	Db	Eb	F	Gb	A♮	Bb	C	Db
Root...	Bb	C	Db	Eb	F	Gb	A♮	Bb

♫ Any extension or extensions may be voiced with the given seventh chord.

Sevenths
DIATONIC CHORD STRUCTURE

	$i^{\triangle 7}$	$ii^{\emptyset 7}$	$III^{+\triangle 7}$	iv^{7}	V^{7}	$VI^{\triangle 7}$	$vii^{\circ 7}$	$i^{\triangle 7}$
7th	A♮	Bb	C	Db	Eb	F	Gb	A♮
5th ...	F	Gb	A♮	Bb	C	Db	Eb	F
3rd ...	Db	Eb	F	Gb	A♮	Bb	C	Db
Root...	Bb	C	Db	Eb	F	Gb	A♮	Bb

♫ A seventh chord is commonly voiced using just the root, third & seventh.

A♭ Minor ^{7 Flats}

E♭ Minor ^{6 Flats}

B♭ Minor ^{5 Flats}

F Minor ^{4 Flats}

C Minor ^{3 Flats}

G Minor ^{2 Flats}

D Minor ^{1 Flat}

A Minor ^{0 Flats}

The Key of F Minor

The F harmonic minor scale form uses the notes F, G, A♭, B♭, C, D♭, E♮ & F.

The Key of F Minor

implies -- F, G, Ab, Bb, C, Db & E♮.

Signature

CLEFS & KEY SIGNATURE

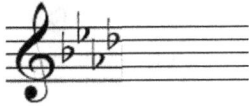

Treble or G clef...

Alto or movable C clef...

Bass or F clef...

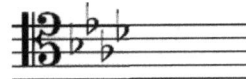

Tenor or movable C clef...

♫ The F minor key signature has four flats -- Bb, Eb, Ab & Db.

Progressions

COMMON PROGRESSIONS

$i \Rightarrow V \Rightarrow i$ ...	implies ...	f min ⇨ C Maj ⇨ f min...
$III^+ \Rightarrow V \Rightarrow i$ ...	implies ...	Ab Aug ⇨ C Maj ⇨ f min...
$i \Rightarrow iv \Rightarrow V \Rightarrow i$ ...	implies ...	f min ⇨ bb min ⇨ C Maj ⇨ f min...
$i \Rightarrow ii° \Rightarrow V \Rightarrow i$ ...	implies ...	f min ⇨ g dim ⇨ C Maj ⇨ f min...
$i \Rightarrow VI \Rightarrow ii° \Rightarrow V$...	implies ...	f min ⇨ Db Maj ⇨ g dim ⇨ C Maj...
$III^+ \Rightarrow VI \Rightarrow ii° \Rightarrow V$...implies ...		Ab Aug ⇨ Db Maj ⇨ g dim ⇨ C Maj...

♫ The primary chords are F minor Tonic, Bb minor Subdominant & C major Dominant.

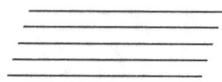

F Triads & Color Tones

The key of A♭ major is...

Color Tones

DIATONIC CHORD STRUCTURE

6th	D♭	E♮	F	G	A♭	B♭	C	D♭
4th	B♭	C	D♭	E♮	F	G	A♭	B♭
2nd	G	A♭	B♭	C	D♭	E♮	F	G
5th ...	C	D♭	E♮	F	G	A♭	B♭	C
3rd ...	A♭	B♭	C	D♭	E♮	F	G	A♭
Root...	F	G	A♭	B♭	C	D♭	E♮	F
	i	ii°	III⁺	iv	V	VI	vii°	i

♪ Any color tone or tones may be voiced with the given triad chord.

Triads

DIATONIC CHORD STRUCTURE

5th ...	C	D♭	E♮	F	G	A♭	B♭	C
3rd ...	A♭	B♭	C	D♭	E♮	F	G	A♭
Root...	F	G	A♭	B♭	C	D♭	E♮	F
	i	ii°	III⁺	iv	V	VI	vii°	i

♪ A triad chord is commonly voiced using just the root & third.

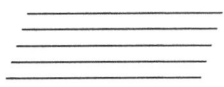

F Sevenths & Extensions

...relative to the key of F minor.

Extensions

DIATONIC CHORD STRUCTURE

13th	Db	E♮	F	G	Ab	Bb	C	Db
11th	Bb	C	Db	E♮	F	G	Ab	Bb
9th	G	Ab	Bb	C	Db	E♮	F	G
7th	E♮	F	G	Ab	Bb	C	Db	E♮
5th ...	C	Db	E♮	F	G	Ab	Bb	C
3rd ...	Ab	Bb	C	Db	E♮	F	G	Ab
Root...	F	G	Ab	Bb	C	Db	E♮	F
	$i^{\Delta 7}$	$ii^{\varnothing 7}$	$III^{+\Delta 7}$	iv^{7}	V^{7}	$VI^{\Delta 7}$	$vii^{\circ 7}$	$i^{\Delta 7}$

♪ Any extension or extensions may be voiced with the given seventh chord.

Sevenths

DIATONIC CHORD STRUCTURE

7th	E♮	F	G	Ab	Bb	C	Db	E♮
5th ...	C	Db	E♮	F	G	Ab	Bb	C
3rd ...	Ab	Bb	C	Db	E♮	F	G	Ab
Root...	F	G	Ab	Bb	C	Db	E♮	F
	$i^{\Delta 7}$	$ii^{\varnothing 7}$	$III^{+\Delta 7}$	iv^{7}	V^{7}	$VI^{\Delta 7}$	$vii^{\circ 7}$	$i^{\Delta 7}$

♪ A seventh chord is commonly voiced using just the root, third & seventh.

A♭ Minor ⁷ ᶠˡᵃᵗˢ

E♭ Minor ⁶ ᶠˡᵃᵗˢ

B♭ Minor ⁵ ᶠˡᵃᵗˢ

F Minor ⁴ ᶠˡᵃᵗˢ

C Minor ³ ᶠˡᵃᵗˢ

G Minor ² ᶠˡᵃᵗˢ

D Minor ¹ ᶠˡᵃᵗ

A Minor ⁰ ᶠˡᵃᵗˢ

The Key of C Minor

The C harmonic minor scale form uses the notes C, D, E♭, F, G, A♭, B♮ & C.

The Key of C Minor

implies -- C, D, Eb, F, G, Ab & Bb.

Signature

CLEFS & KEY SIGNATURE

Treble or G clef...

Alto or movable C clef...

Bass or F clef...

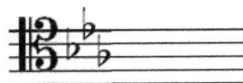

Tenor or movable C clef...

♪ The C minor key signature has three flats -- Bb, Eb & Ab.

Progressions

COMMON PROGRESSIONS

$i \Rightarrow V \Rightarrow i$ ...	implies	...	c min ⇨ G Maj ⇨ c min...
$III^+ \Rightarrow V \Rightarrow i$ ...	implies	...	Eb Aug ⇨ G Maj ⇨ c min...
$i \Rightarrow iv \Rightarrow V \Rightarrow i$ ...	implies	...	c min ⇨ f min ⇨ G Maj ⇨ c min...
$i \Rightarrow ii° \Rightarrow V \Rightarrow i$ ...	implies	...	c min ⇨ d dim ⇨ G Maj ⇨ c min...
$i \Rightarrow VI \Rightarrow ii° \Rightarrow V$ ...	implies	...	c min ⇨ Ab Maj ⇨ d dim ⇨ G Maj...
$III^+ \Rightarrow VI \Rightarrow ii° \Rightarrow V$ ...	implies	...	Eb Aug ⇨ Ab Maj ⇨ d dim ⇨ G Maj...

♪ The primary chords are C minor ^{Tonic}, F minor ^{Subdominant} & G major ^{Dominant}.

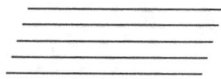

C Triads & Color Tones

The key of Eb major is...

Color Tones

DIATONIC CHORD STRUCTURE

6th	A♭	B♮	C	D	E♭	F	G	A♭
4th	F	G	A♭	B♮	C	D	E♭	F
2nd	D	E♭	F	G	A♭	B♮	C	D
5th ...	G	A♭	B♮	C	D	E♭	F	G
3rd ...	E♭	F	G	A♭	B♮	C	D	E♭
Root...	C	D	E♭	F	G	A♭	B♮	C
	i	ii°	III⁺	iv	V	VI	vii°	i

♫ Any color tone or tones may be voiced with the given triad chord.

Triads

DIATONIC CHORD STRUCTURE

5th ...	G	A♭	B♮	C	D	E♭	F	G
3rd ...	E♭	F	G	A♭	B♮	C	D	E♭
Root...	C	D	E♭	F	G	A♭	B♮	C
	i	ii°	III⁺	iv	V	VI	vii°	i

♫ A triad chord is commonly voiced using just the root & third.

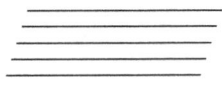

C Sevenths & Extensions

...relative to the key of C minor.

Extensions
DIATONIC CHORD STRUCTURE

13th	Ab	B♮	C	D	Eb	F	G	Ab
11th	F	G	Ab	B♮	C	D	Eb	F
9th	D	Eb	F	G	Ab	B♮	C	D
7th	B♮	C	D	Eb	F	G	Ab	B♮
5th ...	G	Ab	B♮	C	D	Eb	F	G
3rd ...	Eb	F	G	Ab	B♮	C	D	Eb
Root...	C	D	Eb	F	G	Ab	B♮	C
	$i^{\Delta 7}$	$ii^{\varnothing 7}$	$III^{+\Delta 7}$	iv^{7}	V^{7}	$VI^{\Delta 7}$	$vii^{\circ 7}$	$i^{\Delta 7}$

♪ Any extension or extensions may be voiced with the given seventh chord.

Sevenths
DIATONIC CHORD STRUCTURE

7th	B♮	C	D	Eb	F	G	Ab	B♮
5th ...	G	Ab	B♮	C	D	Eb	F	G
3rd ...	Eb	F	G	Ab	B♮	C	D	Eb
Root...	C	D	Eb	F	G	Ab	B♮	C
	$i^{\Delta 7}$	$ii^{\varnothing 7}$	$III^{+\Delta 7}$	iv^{7}	V^{7}	$VI^{\Delta 7}$	$vii^{\circ 7}$	$i^{\Delta 7}$

♪ A seventh chord is commonly voiced using just the root, third & seventh.

UNABRIDGED DIATONICS™   A COMPLETE DIATONIC REFERENCE – THE CIRCLE OF FIFTHS   COPYRIGHT © 2011 OMNI MUSIC PRESS®

Ab Minor ⁷ Flats

Eb Minor ⁶ Flats

Bb Minor ⁵ Flats

F Minor ⁴ Flats

C Minor ³ Flats

G Minor ² Flats

D Minor ¹ Flat

A Minor ⁰ Flats

The Key of G Minor

The G harmonic minor scale form uses the notes G, A, Bb, C, D, Eb, F# & G.

The Key of G Minor

implies -- G, A, B♭, C, D, E♭ & F♯.

Signature

CLEFS & KEY SIGNATURE

Treble or G clef...

Alto or movable C clef...

Bass or F clef...

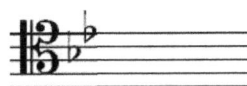

Tenor or movable C clef...

♪ The G minor key signature has two flats -- B♭ & E♭.

Progressions

COMMON PROGRESSIONS

$i \Rightarrow V \Rightarrow i$ ...	implies ...	g min ⇨ D Maj ⇨ g min...
$III^+ \Rightarrow V \Rightarrow i$ ...	implies ...	B♭ Aug ⇨ D Maj ⇨ g min...
$i \Rightarrow iv \Rightarrow V \Rightarrow i$ ...	implies ...	g min ⇨ c min ⇨ D Maj ⇨ g min...
$i \Rightarrow ii° \Rightarrow V \Rightarrow i$ ...	implies ...	g min ⇨ a dim ⇨ D Maj ⇨ g min...
$i \Rightarrow VI \Rightarrow ii° \Rightarrow V$ ...	implies ...	g min ⇨ E♭ Maj ⇨ a dim ⇨ D Maj...
$III^+ \Rightarrow VI \Rightarrow ii° \Rightarrow V$ ...	implies ...	B♭ Aug ⇨ E♭ Maj ⇨ a dim ⇨ D Maj...

♪ The primary chords are G minor ^{Tonic}, C minor ^{Subdominant} & D major ^{Dominant}.

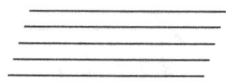

G Triads & Color Tones

The key of B♭ major is...

Color Tones

DIATONIC CHORD STRUCTURE

6th	E♭	F♯	G	A	B♭	C	D	E♭
4th	C	D	E♭	F♯	G	A	B♭	C
2nd	A	B♭	C	D	E♭	F♯	G	A
5th ...	D	E♭	F♯	G	A	B♭	C	D
3rd ...	B♭	C	D	E♭	F♯	G	A	B♭
Root...	G	A	B♭	C	D	E♭	F♯	G
	i	ii°	III+	iv	V	VI	vii°	i

♪ Any color tone or tones may be voiced with the given triad chord.

Triads

DIATONIC CHORD STRUCTURE

5th ...	D	E♭	F♯	G	A	B♭	C	D
3rd ...	B♭	C	D	E♭	F♯	G	A	B♭
Root...	G	A	B♭	C	D	E♭	F♯	G
	i	ii°	III+	iv	V	VI	vii°	i

♪ A triad chord is commonly voiced using just the root & third.

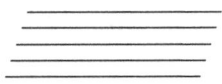

G Sevenths & Extensions

...relative to the key of G minor.

Extensions
DIATONIC CHORD STRUCTURE

13th	E♭	F♯	G	A	B♭	C	D	E♭
11th	C	D	E♭	F♯	G	A	B♭	C
9th	A	B♭	C	D	E♭	F♯	G	A
7th	F♯	G	A	B♭	C	D	E♭	F♯
5th ...	D	E♭	F♯	G	A	B♭	C	D
3rd ...	B♭	C	D	E♭	F♯	G	A	B♭
Root...	G	A	B♭	C	D	E♭	F♯	G
	$i^{\triangle 7}$	$ii^{\varnothing 7}$	$III^{+\triangle 7}$	iv^{7}	V^{7}	$VI^{\triangle 7}$	$vii^{\circ 7}$	$i^{\triangle 7}$

♫ Any extension or extensions may be voiced with the given seventh chord.

Sevenths
DIATONIC CHORD STRUCTURE

7th	F♯	G	A	B♭	C	D	E♭	F♯
5th ...	D	E♭	F♯	G	A	B♭	C	D
3rd ...	B♭	C	D	E♭	F♯	G	A	B♭
Root...	G	A	B♭	C	D	E♭	F♯	G
	$i^{\triangle 7}$	$ii^{\varnothing 7}$	$III^{+\triangle 7}$	iv^{7}	V^{7}	$VI^{\triangle 7}$	$vii^{\circ 7}$	$i^{\triangle 7}$

♫ A seventh chord is commonly voiced using just the root, third & seventh.

Ab Minor ⁷ Flats

Eb Minor ⁶ Flats

Bb Minor ⁵ Flats

F Minor ⁴ Flats

C Minor ³ Flats

G Minor ² Flats

D Minor ¹ Flat

A Minor ⁰ Flats

The Key of D Minor

The D harmonic minor scale form uses the notes D, E, F, G, A, Bb, C# & D.

The Key of D Minor

implies -- D, E, F, G, A, B♭ & C♯.

Signature

CLEFS & KEY SIGNATURE

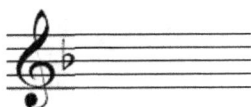

Treble or G clef...

Alto or movable C clef...

Bass or F clef...

Tenor or movable C clef...

♪ The D minor key signature has one flat -- B♭.

Progressions

COMMON PROGRESSIONS

$i \Rightarrow V \Rightarrow i$ ...	implies	...	d min ⇨ A Maj ⇨ d min...
$III^+ \Rightarrow V \Rightarrow i$ ...	implies	...	F Aug ⇨ A Maj ⇨ d min...
$i \Rightarrow iv \Rightarrow V \Rightarrow i$ ...	implies	...	d min ⇨ g min ⇨ A Maj ⇨ d min...
$i \Rightarrow ii° \Rightarrow V \Rightarrow i$ ...	implies	...	d min ⇨ e dim ⇨ A Maj ⇨ d min...
$i \Rightarrow VI \Rightarrow ii° \Rightarrow V$...	implies	...	d min ⇨ B♭ Maj ⇨ e dim ⇨ A Maj...
$III^+ \Rightarrow VI \Rightarrow ii° \Rightarrow V$...implies		...	F Aug ⇨ B♭ Maj ⇨ e dim ⇨ A Maj...

♪ The primary chords are **D minor** Tonic, **G minor** Subdominant & **A major** Dominant.

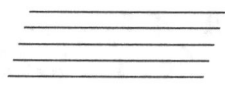

D Triads & Color Tones

The key of F major is...

Color Tones

DIATONIC CHORD STRUCTURE

6th	Bb	C#	D	E	F	G	A	Bb
4th	G	A	Bb	C#	D	E	F	G
2nd	E	F	G	A	Bb	C#	D	E
5th ...	A	Bb	C#	D	E	F	G	A
3rd ...	F	G	A	Bb	C#	D	E	F
Root...	D	E	F	G	A	Bb	C#	D
	i	ii°	III+	iv	V	VI	vii°	i

♫ Any color tone or tones may be voiced with the given triad chord.

Triads

DIATONIC CHORD STRUCTURE

5th ...	A	Bb	C#	D	E	F	G	A
3rd ...	F	G	A	Bb	C#	D	E	F
Root...	D	E	F	G	A	Bb	C#	D
	i	ii°	III+	iv	V	VI	vii°	i

♫ A triad chord is commonly voiced using just the root & third.

D Sevenths & Extensions

...relative to the key of D minor.

E x t e n s i o n s

DIATONIC CHORD STRUCTURE

	$i^{\triangle 7}$	$ii^{\varnothing 7}$	$III^{+\triangle 7}$	iv^{7}	V^{7}	$VI^{\triangle 7}$	$vii^{\circ 7}$	$i^{\triangle 7}$
13th	B♭	C♯	D	E	F	G	A	B♭
11th	G	A	B♭	C♯	D	E	F	G
9th	E	F	G	A	B♭	C♯	D	E
7th	C♯	D	E	F	G	A	B♭	C♯
5th ...	A	B♭	C♯	D	E	F	G	A
3rd ...	F	G	A	B♭	C♯	D	E	F
Root...	D	E	F	G	A	B♭	C♯	D

♪ Any extension or extensions may be voiced with the given seventh chord.

S e v e n t h s

DIATONIC CHORD STRUCTURE

	$i^{\triangle 7}$	$ii^{\varnothing 7}$	$III^{+\triangle 7}$	iv^{7}	V^{7}	$VI^{\triangle 7}$	$vii^{\circ 7}$	$i^{\triangle 7}$
7th	C♯	D	E	F	G	A	B♭	C♯
5th ...	A	B♭	C♯	D	E	F	G	A
3rd ...	F	G	A	B♭	C♯	D	E	F
Root...	D	E	F	G	A	B♭	C♯	D

♪ A seventh chord is commonly voiced using just the root, third & seventh.

133

Ab Minor ^{7 Flats}

Eb Minor ^{6 Flats}

Bb Minor ^{5 Flats}

F Minor ^{4 Flats}

C Minor ^{3 Flats}

G Minor ^{2 Flats}

D Minor ^{1 Flat}

A Minor ^{0 Flats}

The Key of A Minor

The A harmonic minor scale form uses the notes A, B, C, D, E, F, G# & A.

Ab Minor [7 Flats]

Eb Minor [6 Flats]

Bb Minor [5 Flats]

F Minor [4 Flats]

C Minor [3 Flats]

G Minor [2 Flats]

D Minor [1 Flat]

A Minor [0 Flats]

The Key of A Minor

The A harmonic minor scale form uses the notes A, B, C, D, E, F, G# & A.

The Key of A Minor

implies -- A, B, C, D, E, F & G♯.

Signature

CLEFS & KEY SIGNATURE

Treble or G clef...

Alto or movable C clef...

Bass or F clef...

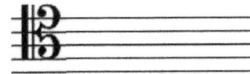

Tenor or movable C clef...

♫ The A minor key signature has no sharps or flats.

Progressions

COMMON PROGRESSIONS

$i \Rightarrow V \Rightarrow i \ldots$	implies	...	a min ⇨ E Maj ⇨ a min...
$III^+ \Rightarrow V \Rightarrow i \ldots$	implies	...	C Aug ⇨ E Maj ⇨ a min...
$i \Rightarrow iv \Rightarrow V \Rightarrow i \ldots$	implies	...	a min ⇨ d min ⇨ E Maj ⇨ a min...
$i \Rightarrow ii° \Rightarrow V \Rightarrow i \ldots$	implies	...	a min ⇨ b dim ⇨ E Maj ⇨ a min...
$i \Rightarrow VI \Rightarrow ii° \Rightarrow V \ldots$	implies	...	a min ⇨ F Maj ⇨ b dim ⇨ E Maj...
$III^+ \Rightarrow VI \Rightarrow ii° \Rightarrow V \ldots$	implies	...	C Aug ⇨ F Maj ⇨ b dim ⇨ E Maj...

♫ The primary chords are A minor ^{Tonic}, D minor ^{Subdominant} & E major ^{Dominant}.

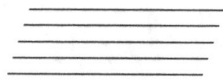

A Triads & Color Tones

The key of C major is...

Color Tones

DIATONIC CHORD STRUCTURE

6th	F	G#	A	B	C	D	E	F
4th	D	E	F	G#	A	B	C	D
2nd	B	C	D	E	F	G#	A	B
5th ...	E	F	G#	A	B	C	D	E
3rd ...	C	D	E	F	G#	A	B	C
Root...	A	B	C	D	E	F	G#	A
	i	*ii°*	*III⁺*	*iv*	*V*	*VI*	*vii°*	*i*

♫ Any color tone or tones may be voiced with the given triad chord.

Triads

DIATONIC CHORD STRUCTURE

5th ...	E	F	G#	A	B	C	D	E
3rd ...	C	D	E	F	G#	A	B	C
Root...	A	B	C	D	E	F	G#	A
	i	*ii°*	*III⁺*	*iv*	*V*	*VI*	*vii°*	*i*

♫ A triad chord is commonly voiced using just the root & third.

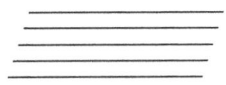

A Sevenths & Extensions

...relative to the key of A minor.

E x t e n s i o n s
DIATONIC CHORD STRUCTURE

	$i^{\triangle 7}$	$ii^{\varnothing 7}$	$III^{+\triangle 7}$	iv^7	V^7	$VI^{\triangle 7}$	$vii^{\circ 7}$	$i^{\triangle 7}$
13th	F	G♯	A	B	C	D	E	F
11th	D	E	F	G♯	A	B	C	D
9th	B	C	D	E	F	G♯	A	B
7th	G♯	A	B	C	D	E	F	G♯
5th ...	E	F	G♯	A	B	C	D	E
3rd ...	C	D	E	F	G♯	A	B	C
Root...	A	B	C	D	E	F	G♯	A

♪ Any extension or extensions may be voiced with the given seventh chord.

S e v e n t h s
DIATONIC CHORD STRUCTURE

	$i^{\triangle 7}$	$ii^{\varnothing 7}$	$III^{+\triangle 7}$	iv^7	V^7	$VI^{\triangle 7}$	$vii^{\circ 7}$	$i^{\triangle 7}$
7th	G♯	A	B	C	D	E	F	G♯
5th ...	E	F	G♯	A	B	C	D	E
3rd ...	C	D	E	F	G♯	A	B	C
Root...	A	B	C	D	E	F	G♯	A

♪ A seventh chord is commonly voiced using just the root, third & seventh.

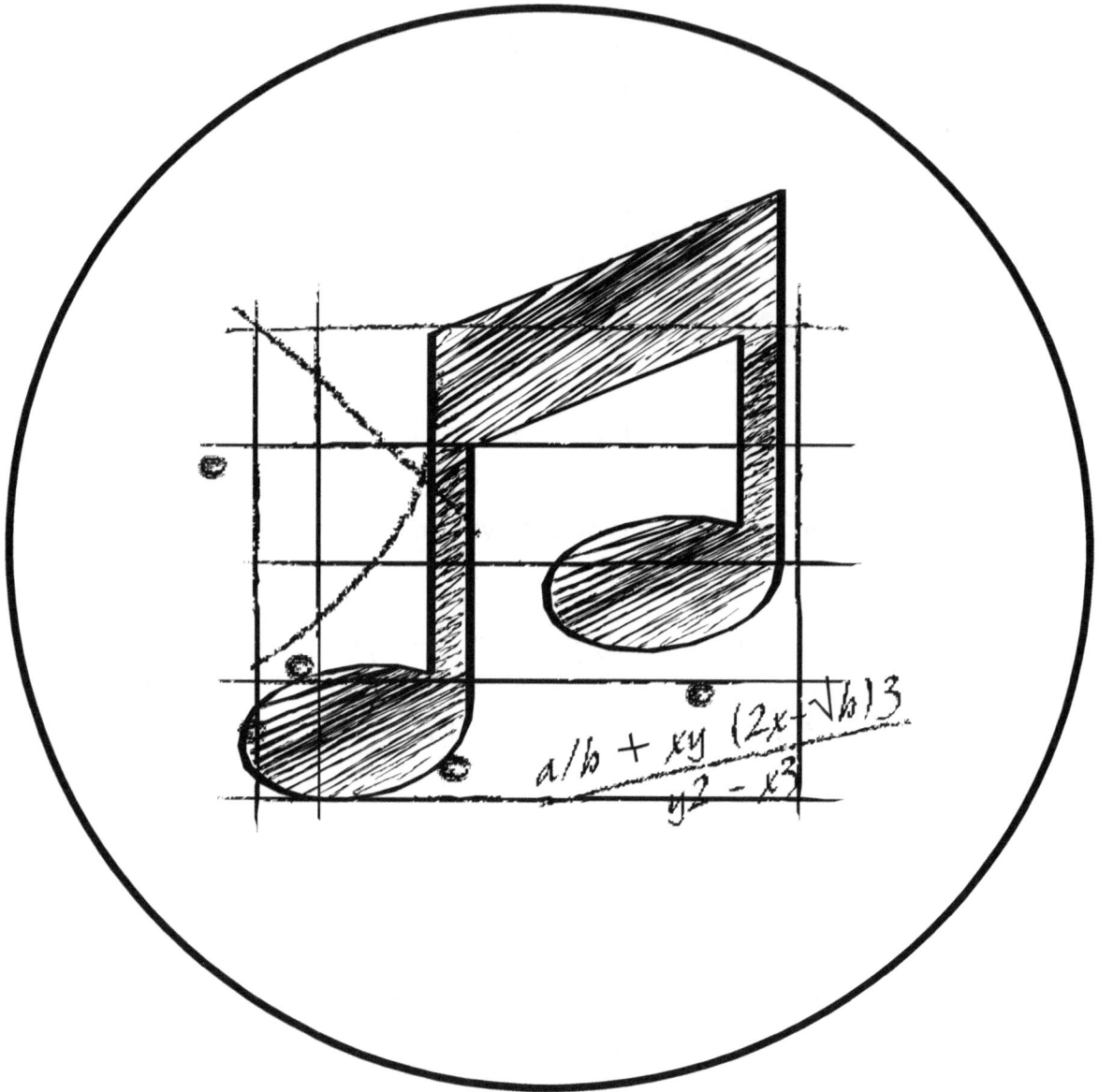

A P P E N D I X   O N E

The Sharp Major Keys

Key of C Major

Key of G Major

Key of D Major

Key of A Major

Key of E Major

Key of B Major

Key of F♯ Major

Key of C♯ Major

C Major
DIATONIC CHORD STRUCTURE

	I	ii	iii	IV	V	vi	vii°	I
6th/13th	A	B	C	D	E	F	G	A
4th/11th	F	G	A	B	C	D	E	F
2nd/9th	D	E	F	G	A	B	C	D
/7th	B	C	D	E	F	G	A	B
5th ...	G	A	B	C	D	E	F	G
3rd ...	E	F	G	A	B	C	D	E
Root...	C	D	E	F	G	A	B	C
	I	ii	iii	IV	V	vi	vii°	I

♫ The primary chords are C major Tonic, F major Subdominant & G major Dominant.

G Major F♯
DIATONIC CHORD STRUCTURE

	I	ii	iii	IV	V	vi	vii°	I
6th/13th	E	F♯	G	A	B	C	D	E
4th/11th	C	D	E	F♯	G	A	B	C
2nd/9th	A	B	C	D	E	F♯	G	A
/7th	F♯	G	A	B	C	D	E	F♯
5th ...	D	E	F♯	G	A	B	C	D
3rd ...	B	C	D	E	F♯	G	A	B
Root...	G	A	B	C	D	E	F♯	G
	I	ii	iii	IV	V	vi	vii°	I

♫ The primary chords are G major Tonic, C major Subdominant & D major Dominant.

D Major F♯ C♯

DIATONIC CHORD STRUCTURE

6th/13th	B	C♯	D	E	F♯	G	A	B
4th/11th	G	A	B	C♯	D	E	F♯	G
2nd/9th	E	F♯	G	A	B	C♯	D	E
/7th	C♯	D	E	F♯	G	A	B	C♯
5th ...	A	B	C♯	D	E	F♯	G	A
3rd ...	F♯	G	A	B	C♯	D	E	F♯
Root...	D	E	F♯	G	A	B	C♯	D
	I	ii	iii	IV	V	vi	vii°	I

♪ The primary chords are D major ᵀᵒⁿⁱᶜ, G major ˢᵘᵇᵈᵒᵐⁱⁿᵃⁿᵗ & A major ᴰᵒᵐⁱⁿᵃⁿᵗ.

A Major F♯ C♯ G♯

DIATONIC CHORD STRUCTURE

6th/13th	F♯	G♯	A	B	C♯	D	E	C♯
4th/11th	D	E	F♯	G♯	A	B	C♯	D
2nd/9th	B	C♯	D	E	F♯	G♯	A	F♯
/7th	G♯	A	B	C♯	D	E	F♯	G♯
5th ...	E	F♯	G♯	A	B	C♯	D	E
3rd ...	C♯	D	E	F♯	G♯	A	B	C♯
Root...	A	B	C♯	D	E	F♯	G♯	A
	I	ii	iii	IV	V	vi	vii°	I

♪ The primary chords are A major ᵀᵒⁿⁱᶜ, D major ˢᵘᵇᵈᵒᵐⁱⁿᵃⁿᵗ & E major ᴰᵒᵐⁱⁿᵃⁿᵗ.

E Major ^{F# C# G# D#}

DIATONIC CHORD STRUCTURE

6th/13th	C#	D#	E	F#	G#	A	B	C#
4th/11th	A	B	C#	D#	E	F#	G#	A
2nd/9th	F#	G#	A	B	C#	D#	E	F#
/7th	D#	E	F#	G#	A	B	C#	D#
5th ...	B	C#	D#	E	F#	G#	A	B
3rd ...	G#	A	B	C#	D#	E	F#	G#
Root...	E	F#	G#	A	B	C#	D#	E
	I	*ii*	*iii*	*IV*	*V*	*vi*	*vii°*	*I*

♫ The primary chords are E major ^{Tonic}, A major ^{Subdominant} & B major ^{Dominant}.

B Major ^{F# C# G# D# A#}

DIATONIC CHORD STRUCTURE

6th/13th	G#	A#	B	C#	D#	E	F#	G#
4th/11th	E	F#	G#	A#	B	C#	D#	E
2nd/9th	C#	D#	E	F#	G#	A#	B	C#
/7th	A#	B	C#	D#	E	F#	G#	A#
5th ...	F#	G#	A#	B	C#	D#	E	F#
3rd ...	D#	E	F#	G#	A#	B	C#	D#
Root...	B	C#	D#	E	F#	G#	A#	B
	I	*ii*	*iii*	*IV*	*V*	*vi*	*vii°*	*I*

♫ The primary chords are B major ^{Tonic}, E major ^{Subdominant} & F# major ^{Dominant}.

F# Major F# C# G# D# A# E#

DIATONIC CHORD STRUCTURE

6th/13th	D#	E#	F#	G#	A#	B	C#	D#
4th/11th	B	C#	D#	E#	F#	G#	A#	B
2nd/9th	G#	A#	B	C#	D#	E#	F#	G#
/7th	E#	F#	G#	A#	B	C#	D#	E#
5th ...	C#	D#	E#	F#	G#	A#	B	C#
3rd ...	A#	B	C#	D#	E#	F#	G#	A#
Root...	F#	G#	A#	B	C#	D#	E#	F#
	I	*ii*	*iii*	*IV*	*V*	*vi*	*vii°*	*I*

♪ The primary chords are F# major ᵀᵒⁿⁱᶜ, B major ˢᵘᵇᵈᵒᵐⁱⁿᵃⁿᵗ & C# major ᴰᵒᵐⁱⁿᵃⁿᵗ.

C# Major F# C# G# D# A# E# B#

DIATONIC CHORD STRUCTURE

6th/13th	A#	B#	C#	D#	E#	F#	G#	A#
4th/11th	F#	G#	A#	B#	C#	D#	E#	F#
2nd/9th	D#	E#	F#	G#	A#	B#	C#	D#
/7th	B#	C#	D#	E#	F#	G#	A#	B#
5th ...	G#	A#	B#	C#	D#	E#	F#	G#
3rd ...	E#	F#	G#	A#	B#	C#	D#	E#
Root...	C#	D#	E#	F#	G#	A#	B#	C#
	I	*ii*	*iii*	*IV*	*V*	*vi*	*vii°*	*I*

♪ The primary chords are C# major ᵀᵒⁿⁱᶜ, F# major ˢᵘᵇᵈᵒᵐⁱⁿᵃⁿᵗ & G# major ᴰᵒᵐⁱⁿᵃⁿᵗ.

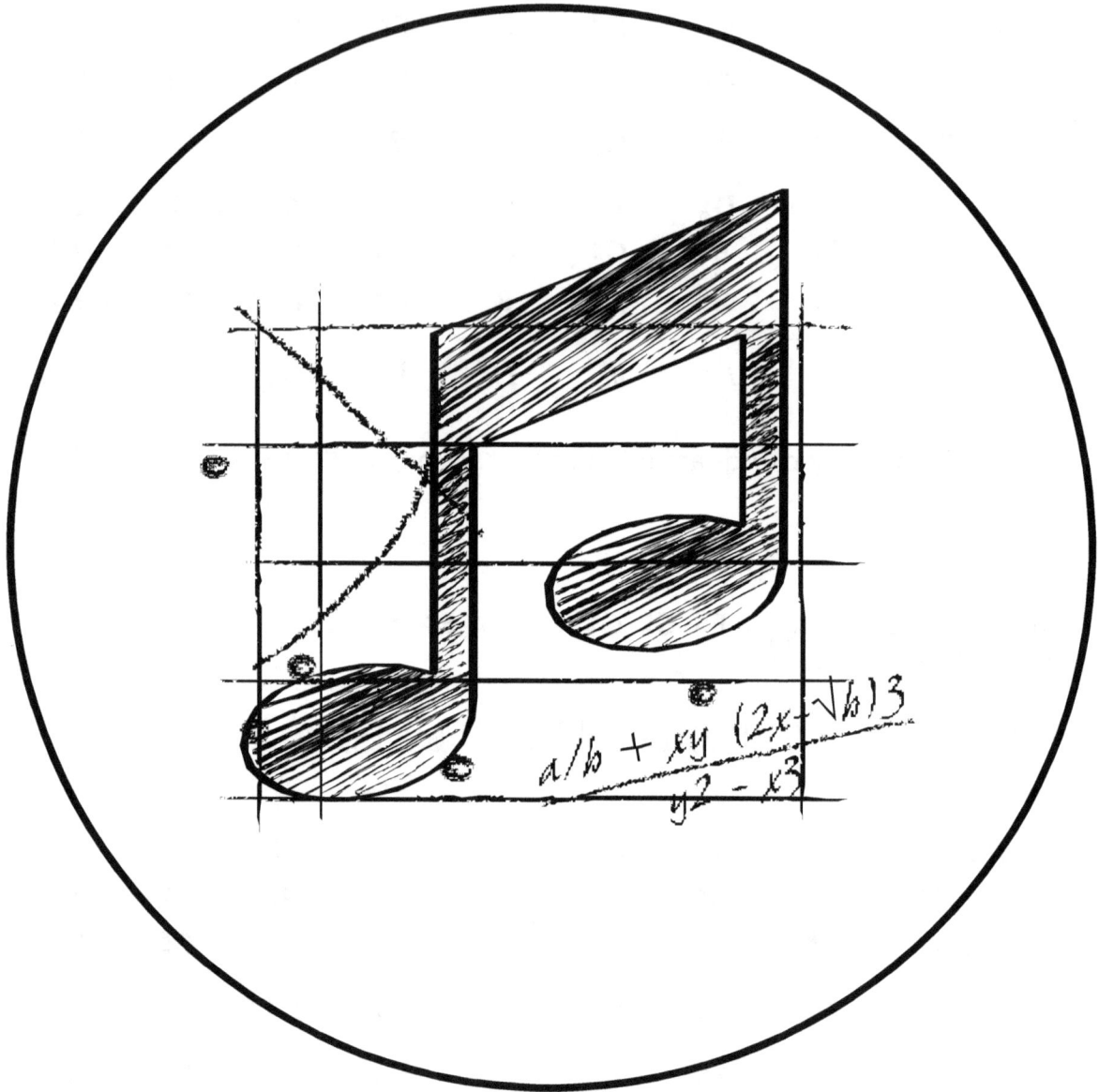

APPENDIX TWO

The Flat Major Keys

C♭ Major B♭ E♭ A♭ D♭ G♭ C♭ F♭

DIATONIC CHORD STRUCTURE

	I	ii	iii	IV	V	vi	vii°	I
6th/13th	A♭	B♭	C♭	D♭	E♭	F♭	G♭	A♭
4th/11th	F♭	G♭	A♭	B♭	C♭	D♭	E♭	F♭
2nd/9th	D♭	E♭	F♭	G♭	A♭	B♭	C♭	D♭
/7th	B♭	C♭	D♭	E♭	F♭	G♭	A♭	B♭
5th ...	G♭	A♭	B♭	C♭	D♭	E♭	F♭	G♭
3rd ...	E♭	F♭	G♭	A♭	B♭	C♭	D♭	E♭
Root...	C♭	D♭	E♭	F♭	G♭	A♭	B♭	C♭
	I	ii	iii	IV	V	vi	vii°	I

♪ The primary chords are C♭ major ^{Tonic}, F♭ major ^{Subdominant} & G♭ major ^{Dominant}.

G♭ Major B♭ E♭ A♭ D♭ G♭ C♭

DIATONIC CHORD STRUCTURE

	I	ii	iii	IV	V	vi	vii°	I
13th	E♭	F	G♭	A♭	B♭	C♭	D♭	E♭
11th	C♭	D♭	E♭	F	G♭	A♭	B♭	C♭
9th	A♭	B♭	C♭	D♭	E♭	F	G♭	A♭
7th	F	G♭	A♭	B♭	C♭	D♭	E♭	F
5th ...	D♭	E♭	F	G♭	A♭	B♭	C♭	D♭
3rd ...	B♭	C♭	D♭	E♭	F	G♭	A♭	B♭
Root...	G♭	A♭	B♭	C♭	D♭	E♭	F	G♭
	I	ii	iii	IV	V	vi	vii°	I

♪ The primary chords are G♭ major ^{Tonic}, C♭ major ^{Subdominant} & D♭ major ^{Dominant}.

D♭ Major ^{B♭ E♭ A♭ D♭ G♭}

DIATONIC CHORD STRUCTURE

6th/13th	B♭	C	D♭	E♭	F	G♭	A♭	B♭
4th/11th	G♭	A♭	B♭	C	D♭	E♭	F	G♭
2nd/9th	E♭	F	G♭	A♭	B♭	C	D♭	E♭
/7th	C	D♭	E♭	F	G♭	A♭	B♭	C
5th ...	A♭	B♭	C	D♭	E♭	F	G♭	A♭
3rd ...	F	G♭	A♭	B♭	C	D♭	E♭	F
Root...	D♭	E♭	F	G♭	A♭	B♭	C	D♭
	I	*ii*	*iii*	*IV*	*V*	*vi*	*vii°*	*I*

♪ The primary chords are D♭ major ^{Tonic}, G♭ major ^{Subdominant} & A♭ major ^{Dominant}.

A♭ Major ^{B♭ E♭ A♭ D♭}

DIATONIC CHORD STRUCTURE

6th/13th	F	G	A♭	B♭	C	D♭	E♭	F
4th/11th	D♭	E♭	F	G	A♭	B♭	C	D♭
2nd/9th	B♭	C	D♭	E♭	F	G	A♭	B♭
/7th	G	A♭	B♭	C	D♭	E♭	F	G
5th ...	E♭	F	G	A♭	B♭	C	D♭	E♭
3rd ...	C	D♭	E♭	F	G	A♭	B♭	C
Root...	A♭	B♭	C	D♭	E♭	F	G	A♭
	I	*ii*	*iii*	*IV*	*V*	*vi*	*vii°*	*I*

♪ The primary chords are A♭ major ^{Tonic}, D♭ major ^{Subdominant} & E♭ major ^{Dominant}.

E♭ Major ^{B♭ E♭ A♭}

DIATONIC CHORD STRUCTURE

6th/13th	C	D	E♭	F	G	A♭	B♭	C
4th/11th	A♭	B♭	C	D	E♭	F	G	A♭
2nd/9th	F	G	A♭	B♭	C	D	E♭	F
/7th	D	E♭	F	G	A♭	B♭	C	D
5th ...	B♭	C	D	E♭	F	G	A♭	B♭
3rd ...	G	A♭	B♭	C	D	E♭	F	G
Root...	E♭	F	G	A♭	B♭	C	D	E♭
	I	*ii*	*iii*	*IV*	*V*	*vi*	*vii°*	*I*

♫ The primary chords are E♭ major ^{Tonic}, A♭ major ^{Subdominant} & B♭ major ^{Dominant}.

B♭ Major ^{B♭ E♭}

DIATONIC CHORD STRUCTURE

6th/13th	G	A	B♭	C	D	E♭	F	G
4th/11th	E♭	F	G	A	B♭	C	D	E♭
2nd/9th	C	D	E♭	F	G	A	B♭	C
/7th	A	B♭	C	D	E♭	F	G	A
5th ...	F	G	A	B♭	C	D	E♭	F
3rd ...	D	E♭	F	G	A	B♭	C	D
Root...	B♭	C	D	E♭	F	G	A	B♭
	I	*ii*	*iii*	*IV*	*V*	*vi*	*vii°*	*I*

♫ The primary chords are B♭ major ^{Tonic}, E♭ major ^{Subdominant} & F major ^{Dominant}.

F Major ^{B♭}

DIATONIC CHORD STRUCTURE

6th/13th	D	E	F	G	A	B♭	C	D
4th/11th	B♭	C	D	E	F	G	A	B♭
2nd/9th	G	A	B♭	C	D	E	F	G
/7th	E	F	G	A	B♭	C	D	E
5th ...	C	D	E	F	G	A	B♭	C
3rd ...	A	B♭	C	D	E	F	G	A
Root...	F	G	A	B♭	C	D	E	F
	I	*ii*	*iii*	*IV*	*V*	*vi*	*vii°*	*I*

♫ The primary chords are F major ^{Tonic}, B♭ major ^{Subdominant} & C major ^{Dominant}.

C Major

DIATONIC CHORD STRUCTURE

6th/13th	A	B	C	D	E	F	G	A
4th/11th	F	G	A	B	C	D	E	F
2nd/9th	D	E	F	G	A	B	C	D
/7th	B	C	D	E	F	G	A	B
5th ...	G	A	B	C	D	E	F	G
3rd ...	E	F	G	A	B	C	D	E
Root...	C	D	E	F	G	A	B	C
	I	*ii*	*iii*	*IV*	*V*	*vi*	*vii°*	*I*

♫ The primary chords are C major ^{Tonic}, F major ^{Subdominant} & G major ^{Dominant}.

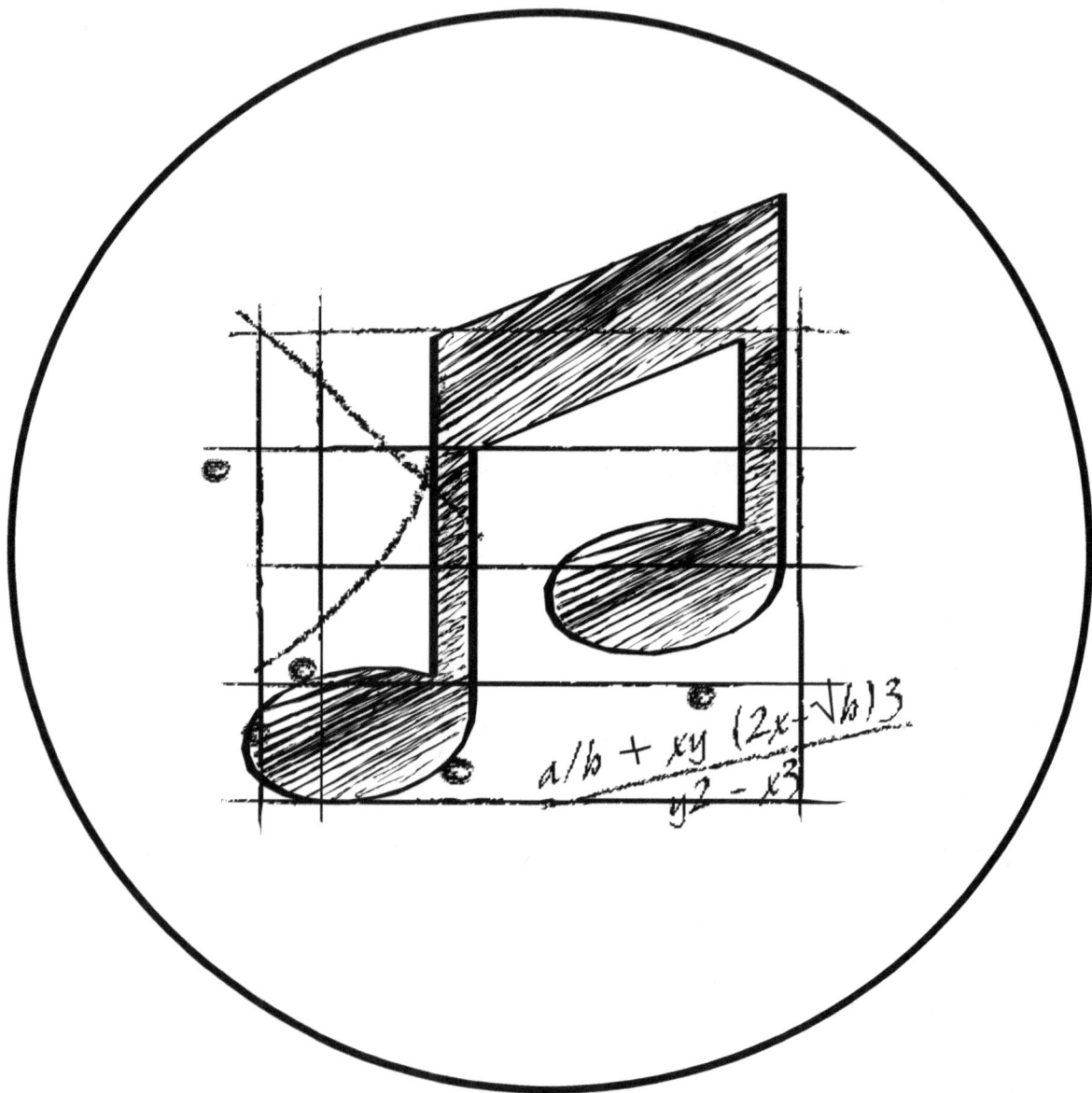

Key of A Minor

Key of E Minor

Key of B Major

Key of F♯ Major

Key of C♯ Major

Key of G♯ Major

Key of D♯ Major

Key of A♯ Major

APPENDIX THREE

The Sharp Minor Keys

A Minor

DIATONIC CHORD STRUCTURE

6th/13th	F	G♯	A	B	C	D	E	F
4th/11th	D	E	F	G♯	A	B	C	D
2nd/9th	B	C	D	E	F	G♯	A	B
/7th	G♯	A	B	C	D	E	F	G♯
5th ...	E	F	G♯	A	B	C	D	E
3rd ...	C	D	E	F	G♯	A	B	C
Root...	A	B	C	D	E	F	G♯	A
	i	*ii*°	*III*⁺	*iv*	*V*	*VI*	*vii*°	*i*

♫ The primary chords are A minor ᵀᵒⁿⁱᶜ, D minor ˢᵘᵇᵈᵒᵐⁱⁿᵃⁿᵗ & E major ᴰᵒᵐⁱⁿᵃⁿᵗ.

E Minor ᶠ♯

DIATONIC CHORD STRUCTURE

6th/13th	C	D♯	E	F♯	G	A	B	C
4th/11th	A	B	C	D♯	E	F♯	G	A
2nd/9th	F♯	G	A	B	C	D♯	E	F♯
/7th	D♯	E	F♯	G	A	B	C	D♯
5th ...	B	C	D♯	E	F♯	G	A	B
3rd ...	G	A	B	C	D♯	E	F♯	G
Root...	E	F♯	G	A	B	C	D♯	E
	i	*ii*°	*III*⁺	*iv*	*V*	*VI*	*vii*°	*i*

♫ The primary chords are E minor ᵀᵒⁿⁱᶜ, A minor ˢᵘᵇᵈᵒᵐⁱⁿᵃⁿᵗ & B major ᴰᵒᵐⁱⁿᵃⁿᵗ.

B Minor ^{F# C#}

DIATONIC CHORD STRUCTURE

6th/13th	G	A#	B	C#	D	E	F#	G
4th/11th	E	F#	G	A#	B	C#	D	E
2nd/9th	C#	D	E	F#	G	A#	B	C#
/7th	A#	B	C#	D	E	F#	G	A#
5th ...	F#	G	A#	B	C#	D	E	F#
3rd ...	D	E	F#	G	A#	B	C#	D
Root...	B	C#	D	E	F#	G	A#	B
	i	*ii*°	*III*⁺	*iv*	*V*	*VI*	*vii*°	*i*

♫ The primary chords are B minor ^{Tonic}, E minor ^{Subdominant} & F# major ^{Dominant}.

F# Minor ^{F# C# G#}

DIATONIC CHORD STRUCTURE

6th/13th	D	E#	F#	G#	A	B	C#	D
4th/11th	B	C#	D	E#	F#	G#	A	B
2nd/9th	G#	A	B	C#	D	E#	F#	G#
/7th	E#	F#	G#	A	B	C#	D	E#
5th ...	C#	D	E#	F#	G#	A	B	C#
3rd ...	A	B	C#	D	E#	F#	G#	A
Root...	F#	G#	A	B	C#	D	E#	F#
	i	*ii*°	*III*⁺	*iv*	*V*	*VI*	*vii*°	*i*

♫ The primary chords are F# minor ^{Tonic}, B minor ^{Subdominant} & C# major ^{Dominant}.

C♯ Minor ^{F♯ C♯ G♯ D♯}

DIATONIC CHORD STRUCTURE

6th/13th	A	B♯	C♯	D♯	E	F♯	G♯	A
4th/11th	F♯	G♯	A	B♯	C♯	D♯	E	F♯
2nd/9th	D♯	E	F♯	G♯	A	B♯	C♯	D♯
/7th	B♯	C♯	D♯	E	F♯	G♯	A	B♯
5th …	G♯	A	B♯	C♯	D♯	E	F♯	G♯
3rd …	E	F♯	G♯	A	B♯	C♯	D♯	E
Root…	C♯	D♯	E	F♯	G♯	A	B♯	C♯
	i	*ii°*	*III⁺*	*iv*	*V*	*VI*	*vii°*	*i*

♫ The primary chords are C♯ minor ^{Tonic}, F♯ minor ^{Subdominant} & G♯ major ^{Dominant}.

G♯ Minor ^{F♯ C♯ G♯ D♯ A♯}

DIATONIC CHORD STRUCTURE

6th/13th	E	F𝄪	G♯	A♯	B	C♯	D♯	E
4th/11th	C♯	D♯	E	F𝄪	G♯	A♯	B	C♯
2nd/9th	A♯	B	C♯	D♯	E	F𝄪	G♯	A♯
/7th	F𝄪	G♯	A♯	B	C♯	D♯	E	F𝄪
5th …	D♯	E	F𝄪	G♯	A♯	B	C♯	D♯
3rd …	B	C♯	D♯	E	F𝄪	G♯	A♯	B
Root…	G♯	A♯	B	C♯	D♯	E	F𝄪	G♯
	i	*ii°*	*III⁺*	*iv*	*V*	*VI*	*vii°*	*i*

♫ The primary chords are G♯ minor ^{Tonic}, C♯ minor ^{Subdominant} & D♯ major ^{Dominant}.

D# Minor F# C# G# D# A# E#

DIATONIC CHORD STRUCTURE

6th/13th	B	C×	D#	E#	F#	G#	A#	B
4th/11th	G#	A#	B	C×	D#	E#	F#	D#
2nd/9th	E#	F#	G#	A#	B	C×	D#	E#
/7th	C×	D#	E#	F#	G#	A#	B	C×
5th ...	A#	B	C×	D#	E#	F#	G#	A#
3rd ...	F#	G#	A#	B	C×	D#	E#	F#
Root...	D#	E#	F#	G#	A#	B	C×	D#
	i	*ii*°	*III*⁺	*iv*	*V*	*VI*	*vii*°	*i*

♪ The primary chords are D# minor ᵀᵒⁿⁱᶜ, G# minor ˢᵘᵇᵈᵒᵐⁱⁿᵃⁿᵗ & A# major ᴰᵒᵐⁱⁿᵃⁿᵗ.

A# Minor F# C# G# D# A# E# B#

DIATONIC CHORD STRUCTURE

6th/13th	F#	G×	A#	B#	C#	D#	E#	F#
4th/11th	D#	E#	F#	G×	A#	B#	C#	D#
2nd/9th	B#	C#	D#	E#	F#	G×	A#	B#
/7th	G×	A#	B#	C#	D#	E#	F#	G×
5th ...	E#	F#	G×	A#	B#	C#	D#	E#
3rd ...	C#	D#	E#	F#	G×	A#	B#	C#
Root...	A#	B#	C#	D#	E#	F#	G×	A#
	i	*ii*°	*III*⁺	*iv*	*V*	*VI*	*vii*°	*i*

♪ The primary chords are A# minor ᵀᵒⁿⁱᶜ, D# minor ˢᵘᵇᵈᵒᵐⁱⁿᵃⁿᵗ & E# major ᴰᵒᵐⁱⁿᵃⁿᵗ.

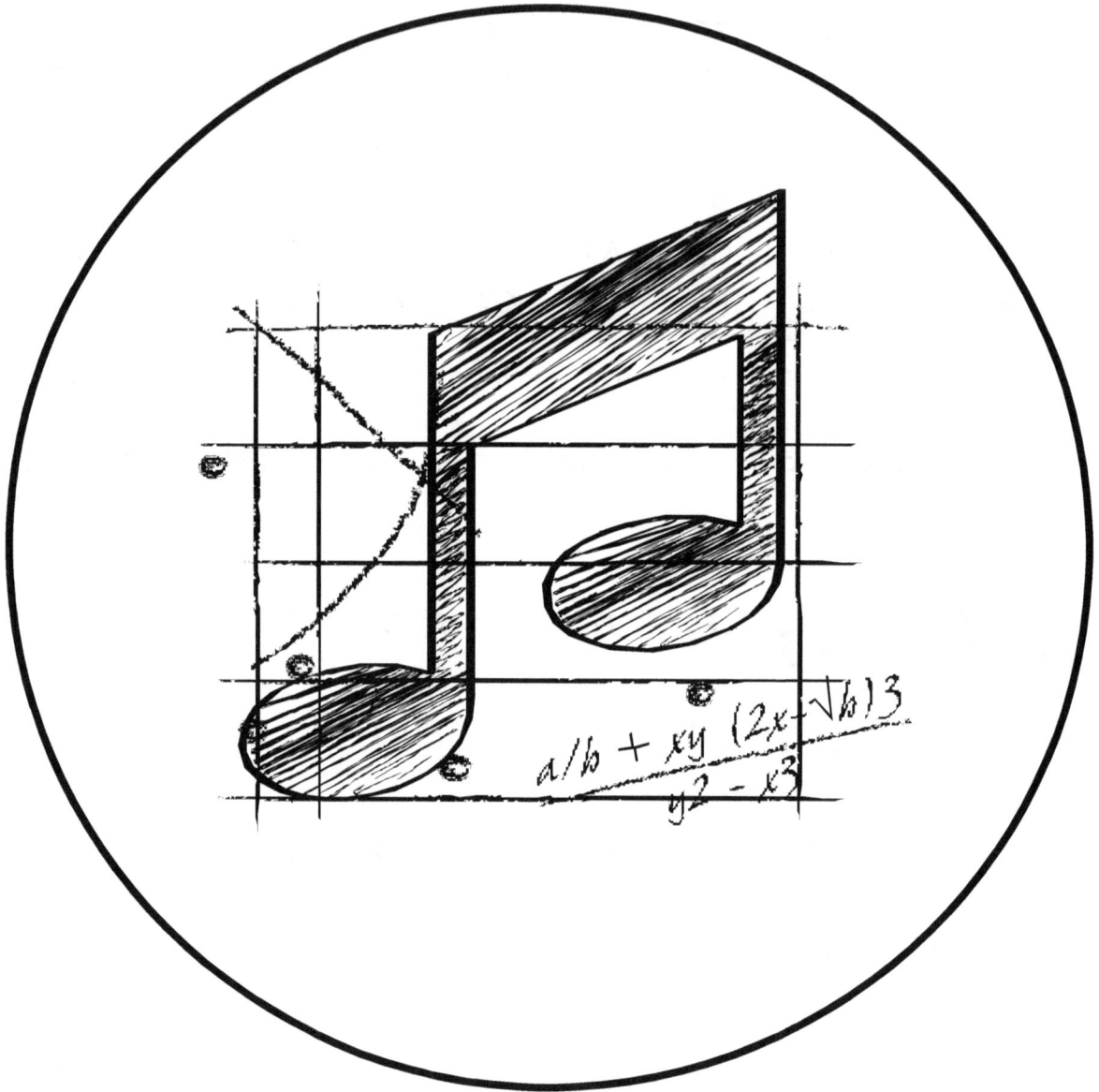

A P P E N D I X   F O U R

♭

The Flat Minor Keys

A♭ Minor B♭ E♭ A♭ D♭ G♭ C♭ F♭

DIATONIC CHORD STRUCTURE

6th/13th	F♭	G♮	A♭	B♭	C♭	D♭	E♭	F♭
4th/11th	D♭	E♭	F♭	G♮	A♭	B♭	C♭	D♭
2nd/9th	B♭	C♭	D♭	E♭	F♭	G♮	A♭	B♭
/7th	G♮	A♭	B♭	C♭	D♭	E♭	F♭	G♮
5th ...	E♭	F♭	G♮	A♭	B♭	C♭	D♭	E♭
3rd ...	C♭	D♭	E♭	F♭	G♮	A♭	B♭	C♭
Root...	A♭	B♭	C♭	D♭	E♭	F♭	G♮	A♭
	i	ii°	III⁺	iv	V	VI	vii°	i

♫ The primary chords are A♭ minor ᵀᵒⁿⁱᶜ, D♭ minor ˢᵘᵇᵈᵒᵐⁱⁿᵃⁿᵗ & E♭ major ᴰᵒᵐⁱⁿᵃⁿᵗ.

E♭ Minor B♭ E♭ A♭ D♭ G♭ C♭

DIATONIC CHORD STRUCTURE

6th/13th	C♭	D♮	E♭	F	G♭	A♭	B♭	C♭
4th/11th	A♭	B♭	C♭	D♮	E♭	F	G♭	A♭
2nd/9th	F	G♭	A♭	B♭	C♭	D♮	E♭	F
/7th	D♮	E♭	F	G♭	A♭	B♭	C♭	D♮
5th ...	B♭	C♭	D♮	E♭	F	G♭	A♭	B♭
3rd ...	G♭	A♭	B♭	C♭	D♮	E♭	F	G♭
Root...	E♭	F	G♭	A♭	B♭	C♭	D♮	E♭
	i	ii°	III⁺	iv	V	VI	vii°	i

♫ The primary chords are E♭ minor ᵀᵒⁿⁱᶜ, A♭ minor ˢᵘᵇᵈᵒᵐⁱⁿᵃⁿᵗ & B♭ major ᴰᵒᵐⁱⁿᵃⁿᵗ.

B♭ Minor B♭ E♭ A♭ D♭ G♭

DIATONIC CHORD STRUCTURE

6th/13th	G♭	A♮	B♭	C	D♭	E♭	F	G♭
4th/11th	E♭	F	G♭	A♮	B♭	C	D♭	E♭
2nd/9th	C	D♭	E♭	F	G♭	A♮	B♭	C
/7th	A♮	B♭	C	D♭	E♭	F	G♭	A♮
5th ...	F	G♭	A♮	B♭	C	D♭	E♭	F
3rd ...	D♭	E♭	F	G♭	A♮	B♭	C	D♭
Root...	B♭	C	D♭	E♭	F	G♭	A♮	B♭
	i	*ii*°	*III*⁺	*iv*	*V*	*VI*	*vii*°	*i*

♪ The primary chords are B♭ minor ^{Tonic}, E♭ minor ^{Subdominant} & F major ^{Dominant}.

F Minor B♭ E♭ A♭ A♭

DIATONIC CHORD STRUCTURE

6th/13th	D♭	E♮	F	G	A♭	B♭	C	D♭
4th/11th	B♭	C	D♭	E♮	F	G	A♭	B♭
2nd/9th	G	A♭	B♭	C	D♭	E♮	F	G
/7th	E♮	F	G	A♭	B♭	C	D♭	E♮
5th ...	C	D♭	E♮	F	G	A♭	B♭	C
3rd ...	A♭	B♭	C	D♭	E♮	F	G	A♭
Root...	F	G	A♭	B♭	C	D♭	E♮	F
	i	*ii*°	*III*⁺	*iv*	*V*	*VI*	*vii*°	*i*

♪ The primary chords are F minor ^{Tonic}, B♭ minor ^{Subdominant} & C major ^{Dominant}.

C Minor ^{B♭ E♭ A♭}

DIATONIC CHORD STRUCTURE

6th/13th	A♭	B♮	C	D	E♭	F	G	A♭
4th/11th	F	G	A♭	B♭	C	D	E♭	F
2nd/9th	D	E♭	F	G	A♭	B♮	C	D
/7th	B♮	C	D	E♭	F	G	A♭	B♮
5th ...	G	A♭	B♮	C	D	E♭	F	G
3rd ...	E♭	F	G	A♭	B♮	C	D	E♭
Root...	C	D	E♭	F	G	A♭	B♮	C
	i	*ii°*	*III⁺*	*iv*	*V*	*VI*	*vii°*	*i*

♪ The primary chords are C minor ^{Tonic}, F minor ^{Subdominant} & G major ^{Dominant}.

G Minor ^{B♭ E♭}

DIATONIC CHORD STRUCTURE

6th/13th	E♭	F♯	G	A	B♭	C	D	E♭
4th/11th	C	D	E♭	F♯	G	A	B♭	C
2nd/9th	A	B♭	C	D	E♭	F♯	G	A
/7th	F♯	G	A	B♭	C	D	E♭	F♯
5th ...	D	E♭	F♯	G	A	B♭	C	D
3rd ...	B♭	C	D	E♭	F♯	G	A	B♭
Root...	G	A	B♭	C	D	E♭	F♯	G
	i	*ii°*	*III⁺*	*iv*	*V*	*VI*	*vii°*	*i*

♪ The primary chords are G minor ^{Tonic}, C minor ^{Subdominant} & D major ^{Dominant}.

D Minor ♭ᵇ

DIATONIC CHORD STRUCTURE

6ᵗʰ/13ᵗʰ	B♭	C♯	D	E	F	G	A	B♭
4ᵗʰ/11ᵗʰ	G	A	B♭	C♯	D	E	F	G
2ⁿᵈ/9ᵗʰ	E	F	G	A	B♭	C♯	D	E
/7ᵗʰ	C♯	D	E	F	G	A	B♭	C♯
5ᵗʰ ...	A	B♭	C♯	D	E	F	G	A
3ʳᵈ ...	F	G	A	B♭	C♯	D	E	F
Root...	D	E	F	G	A	B♭	C♯	D
	i	*ii°*	*III⁺*	*iv*	*V*	*VI*	*vii°*	*i*

♫ The primary chords are D minor ᵀᵒⁿⁱᶜ, G minor ˢᵘᵇᵈᵒᵐⁱⁿᵃⁿᵗ & A major ᴰᵒᵐⁱⁿᵃⁿᵗ.

A Minor

DIATONIC CHORD STRUCTURE

6ᵗʰ/13ᵗʰ	F	G♯	A	B	C	D	E	F
4ᵗʰ/11ᵗʰ	D	E	F	G♯	A	B	C	D
2ⁿᵈ/9ᵗʰ	B	C	D	E	F	G♯	A	B
/7ᵗʰ	G♯	A	B	C	D	E	F	G♯
5ᵗʰ ...	E	F	G♯	A	B	C	D	E
3ʳᵈ ...	C	D	E	F	G♯	A	B	C
Root...	A	B	C	D	E	F	G♯	A
	i	*ii°*	*III⁺*	*iv*	*V*	*VI*	*vii°*	*i*

♫ The primary chords are A minor ᵀᵒⁿⁱᶜ, D minor ˢᵘᵇᵈᵒᵐⁱⁿᵃⁿᵗ & E major ᴰᵒᵐⁱⁿᵃⁿᵗ.